Little Month of St. Joseph

BY THE

REVEREND FATHER MARIN DE BOYLESVE, S. J.

Little Month of St. Joseph

SAINT JOSEPH

ACCORDING TO THE GOSPEL

BY THE

REVEREND FATHER MARIN DE BOYLESVE, S. J.

Meditations and Anecdotes for each Day of the Month of Saint Joseph

WITH PRAYERS AND DEVOTIONS

TRANSLATED BY MRS. EDWARD HAZELAND

Originally published by Burns and Oates, 1886
London and New York

This edition annotated by E.A. Bucchianeri.
Additional traditional devotions
to St. Joseph also included.

Batalha Publishers
Fatima, Portugal

Originally published by Burnes and Oates in 1866 London and New York, reprinted 1886. This reprint edition with biography of the author, annotations and appendix by E.A. Bucchianeri, © 2020-2021 by Batalha Publishers, Portugal. Appendix features traditional Roman Catholic prayers and quotations in the public domain.

ISBN: 978-989-96844-8-5

This new edition:

✠ *Nihil Obstat*. Dec. 2020. Vicar General of the Leiria-Fatima Diocese. Permission granted for publication.

TABLE OF CONTENTS

Prayers to Saint Joseph

APPENDIX

About this Edition

Fr. Marin de Boylesve's devotional book 'Little Month of St. Joseph' was translated into English by Mrs. Edward Hazeland and originally published by the Catholic publishers Burns and Oates in 1866 London and New York. This reprint is from the 1886 edition. While faithful to the original devotional text and its British spelling, this reprint features several changes and additions: biography of the author, a reconstructed Table of Contents, illustrations, larger print and removal of dated punctuation such as commas where required for easier reading, the addition of informative footnotes with explanations not included by Fr. de Boylesve. An Appendix has been added featuring two devotions to St. Joseph referred to by Fr. Boylesve but not included in his original book, also other traditional devotions and prayers to St. Joseph not included in the original.

E.A. Bucchianeri

About the Author

Fr. Marin de Boylesve was born on November 28, 1813 at the Château de la Coltrie in the commune of Saint-Lambert de la Potherie near Angers. He came from a distinguished aristocratic family whose name can be traced back many centuries as seen in Abbé Jean-Baptiste Ladvocat's *Dictionnaire historique portatif* (1755). Fr. Marin descended directly from Eslienne Boyliaue (or Boilyeve), the great statesman and the principal adviser of St. Louis IX, King of France. Other illustrious ancestors included intrepid knights, one in particular also named Marin joined the cause of King Henry IV. After the Battle of Arques, the king called him 'his beloved knight', granted him a heredity knighthood in 1597, then was made Seigneur de la Maurouziere in 1598 thereby granting him the right to add three gold fleur-de-lis to the top of his arms and bear the signs of the Order of St. Michel in his escutcheon. He was also appointed lieutenant-general of Anjou and councillor of state as a reward for his dedication. Another Marin Boylesve appears in the family line, the third to hold the name, and was in service to King Louis XIV as manager of his hôtel. Loyal to the French King and to their Catholic faith, many members of the family were forced to emigrate during the French Revolution, but some members stayed behind in their beloved France. Fr. de Boylesve would recall a favourite family story, of how his grandmother was imprisoned in Angers by the Revolutionaries and managed a daring escape on the road during a prisoner transfer to the local castle. While she pretended to pick up a dropped package, a solider kicked her into the ditch. She took the opportunity to flee to a nearby house. However, when they threatened to imprison those harbouring escaped prisoners, she bravely marched straight in to the Revolutionary Office and gave herself up to ensure the safety of those who sheltered her. The revolutionaries did not dare risk upsetting the populace as her father was the former mayor of Angers before the Revolution and loved by the people. They decided to let her return to her father's house.

Fr. de Boylesve was the last direct descendant of his distinguished line, having followed the call to enter the Company of Jesus, or Jesuits, which also is a remarkable story of a predestined vocation. The Jesuits were persecuted due to fears they were growing in power and wealth. Pressured by the royal courts of Europe, Pope Clement XIV suppressed the Society, forcing members of the order to renounce their vows and go into exile. They were expelled from France in 1764. Fr. de Boylesve's mother, Clémentine de Livonnière, made a solemn promise on the day of her wedding that if God permitted the Jesuits to return to France and she was granted a son, she would offer him to the order and entrust him to it. As mentioned, Fr. Marin was born in 1813, a year before 1814 when Pope Pius VII restored the Society. Tragedy struck when Marin's father died,

Marin was only ten months old at the time, but keeping her promise his mother dutifully sent him for his education at the age of ten to the Jesuit Fathers of Montmorillon. The moment he arrived at the school and saw a Jesuit for the first time who happened to be the Superior of the college Fr. Michel Le Blanc, he heard an inner voice say to him: "Little one, that is what you will be."

Fr. de Boylesve entered the school as a student and was destined never to leave the Jesuits. In 1831 he turned eighteen, a year after the July Revolution of 1830, which saw the rightful king to the French throne Charles X overthrown. His heir, Henry V the 'Miracle Child', was forced into exile at the age of ten, his throne usurped by the man who had been approached to be his regent, Louis-Philippe, Duke of Orléans. The events of the times burned the hearts of the faithful as the historical church of the royal family, Saint-Germain-l'Auxerrois, was profaned. Paris was sacked, and wayside devotional crosses and shrines over large areas of France were destroyed as Catholic legitimist symbols of Charles X, even those which had no royal significance or connection to the king.

Fr. Marin had just completed his schooling when he formally announced his decision to enter the Society, the historic events of the previous year and their aftermath no doubt influencing his decision. Writing to his grandmother he declared:

"The course of my studies completed I could not remain without doing anything. God will ask us for an exact account of all the moments He gives us. Full of this thought I ardently wished to serve my country and the Church especially. At a time when both are in such great peril, as a Frenchman and as a Christian, I felt the need to throw myself into the thick of the fray. To take place in the first rows under the banners of religion whose triumph alone can bring glory and happiness back to my homeland, to serve immediately under my first head Jesus Christ, to be one of His companions, seemed to me the most glorious at the same time as most useful for my neighbour. Immense advantages, treasures of happiness and glory, the hundredfold from this life of all that I would give to the Lord, all of these promised in the gospel by Jesus Christ, strongly attracted me to be generous. What more could I do than give myself? (...)"

His family strongly opposed, especially as he was the last direct heir to the Boylesve house, but his mother let him go despite the great sacrifice, no doubt she understood God was accepting her promise to give him to the Jesuits, and not just for his education but now was asking for his whole life, a bitter dreg for her down to the last drop of the cup.

He entered the Novitiate in 1831 at Estavayer in the canton of Fribourg in Switzerland with two other students. As they arrived at their new school, they rang the doorbell at the moment the house clock struck three. The Father who received them remarked: "You are entering at the hour of the Sacred Heart." This introduction to a new school would once again give Fr. de Boylesve a sign regarding the future work he would one day accomplish, although on this occasion he did not know it at the time. He made his first vows at the Maison du Passage on October 10, 1833. He studied philosophy and then in 1835 became a supervisor at the Collège de Mélan, a position he held for one year. He remained in the same college until 1842 where he was in succession professor of grammar, humanities and rhetoric. He thoroughly enjoyed his work with the students, writing in 1837:

"I find this job a lot of fun, despite the hardships that come with it. I have forty students; I love them and I try to spare nothing to make them good Christians, educated Christians capable of one day rendering true service to religion and to the state. It is the sight of such a noble ending that sustains and animates me." In the same letter he continues, regarding his concern for his family, "(...) what the only important thing is, is everyone behaving well and does he remember the motto of the family, RELIGIO, PATRIA? For me who gave up everything, even my name which will be extinguished in my person, I remember it, and God grant that I am consumed and that I use myself in the service of one and of the other."

Although renouncing his aristocratic life he never gave up its noble spirit represented by the family motto, an ardent loyalty to the Catholic faith of his forefathers and his country. In the title pages of his texts he included the family crest of three crosses and motto: RELIGIO, PATRIE –

"Faith and Country". Those who knew him and his 'military' style ways said he was just like the loyal intrepid knights of old.

At the end of 1842 he returned to France. He took theology courses at Laval for four years. Instinctively he was drawn to the writings of St. Thomas Aquinas and steered clear of new systems that deviated from the philosophical teachings of the Seraphic Doctor. In 1846 theology training completed, Fr. Boylesve was sent by his superiors to Angers, then in his third year at Notre-Dame d'Ay. In 1848 he was appointed to Brugelette, where he occupied the chair of philosophy. One student who fondly recalled Fr. de Boylesve and his time at Brugelette said his arrival was providential. His classes were easy to follow his manner clear and crisp, but this is not all that gained the respect of the students. In 1848 they were restless as revolution was in the air, Louis-Philippe I, who had overthrown Catholic King Charles X was now in his own turn overthrown. Rising above and beyond what was required of his philosophy courses, Fr. Boylesve seized the opportunity like a knight-commander of old to direct the lazy students yet bursting with energy towards something constructive: Catholic action to fashion them into vigorous young men of service for Church and country. With his apostolic action he captivated the students with his literature classes, speaking on many subjects from philosophy, history, politics both ancient and modern. He particularly drew them with his catechism lessons on the Council of Trent, his clarity and enthusiasm captivating them.

As Fr. de Boylesve loved his students he was equally admired and loved by them, earning the nickname 'The Captain' as a mark of respect. The students composed a military style tune for his birthday, the refrain remaining popular and hummed everywhere: "Courageous Captain, lead us into battle." A student recalls: "I understood all that was apostolic about his action on us. We can sum it up by saying that he made it his mission to preach to us always and everywhere the contemplation of Saint Ignatius on the Reign of Jesus Christ as it is given in the Exercises." In 1851 Fr. Boylesve was sent to Vannes where he was made prefect of studies, his nickname 'The Captain' following him. In October 1853 he left the post and resumed teaching philosophy, a position that he would keep for a long time, either in Poitiers or in Vaugirard.

Known to be quiet and reserved when on his own, it was another matter when he was teaching or publicly speaking. He was incapable of remaining silent or softening his direct manner of expression when it was a question of truth, and did not hold back when it came to defend the Faith and the Church against unbelievers, becoming as noted like his knight-ancestor of old, charging forth to give chase and defeat any bold rascal on the field of battle albeit with his tongue and writings rather than with a literal sword. His attitude is quaintly summed up by the art critique he once gave of the statue of the fountain of St. Michael in Paris, complaining with slight annoyance that the mighty archangel was made to look too carefree and benevolent when dispatching Satan: "See then, it is that he seems to spare him!" He was also a zealous worker and relished activity. He once wrote: "I challenge my superiors to give me too much work." In addition to his religious duties and teaching, he was a prolific writer, his output seeming to have no end. He wrote on a myriad of subjects and in different genres, from devotional booklets and pamphlets to history, literature, philosophy, Biblical dramas, summaries of the Church Fathers and Doctors, his own sermons, studies of the Scriptures, Our Lady, the Exercises of St. Ignatius just to name a few, there were always more plans for further works in progress, his room filled with notes and notebooks. He was always studying as well, also making it a practise to read through the entire Bible every year. One might call him a workaholic in today's terms, but it was noted he believed in a time and a place for everything and diligently managed his hours. He enjoyed recreation time, especially going for walks, and did not sacrifice rest. Despite his zest for work, he disapproved of a few young professors who sacrificed too much sleep and recreation time for their studies, endangering their health. Yet, while sparing of his time, he was ever charitable and ready to help another all for the glory of God.

In September 1870 Fr. de Boylesve was sent to the College of Le Mans, Notre-Dame de Sainte-Croix, when the Franco-Prussian war was raging and France suffered the indignity of invasion. The humiliation felt by the country also struck the pious and patriotic Fr. de Boylesve to the core: "I searched through the memories of my life; I do not remember ever having felt greater pain than this, not even when I learned of my mother's death. This humiliation of France, the eldest daughter of the Church, thus succumbing before Prussia, the eldest daughter of Protestantism, in the face of the whole world, is something unheard of."

The Messenger, the magazine of the Apostleship of Prayer run by the Jesuits, began spreading the visions of St. Margaret Mary, declaring the only way France would be saved from her enemies was to embrace the devotion to the Sacred Heart. The message inspired Fr. de Boylesve. He became a chaplain to the Catholic Papal Zouaves forces sent to defend the French Motherland from the Protestant invaders, giving them rousing sermons: "Clotilde, inspiring faith in Clovis, saved the Franks and slaughtered the Germans at their feet ... Joan of Arc by her standard delivered France from the English! Your standard is the Sacred Heart." The Zouaves placed the Sacred Heart on their banner. Fr. de Boylesve also busily spread Sacred Heart badges of wool for the soldiers to pin on their uniforms, for they were in high demand. A gifted and inspiring preacher, his sermons encouraged them onward, even when they were driven back in defeat by the Prussians to where the soldiers remarked: "This man can lead us to the fire tomorrow; we would gladly be killed for him." No doubt it was through his connection as chaplain to the Zouaves that Fr. de Boylesve heard of the touching story of one of their comrades who had a deep devotion to St. Joseph and obtained the grace to see the saint before his death, which he included in one of the Meditations of the 'Little Month of St. Joseph'.

Fr. de Boylesve is fondly remembered today in Catholic circles in France for his work as the director of the Apostleship of Prayer in Le Mans through which he contributed to the spread of devotion to the Sacred Heart. On October 17, 1870 Fr de Boylesve was appointed to preach at the Visitation of Le Mans upon St. Margaret Mary for his subject, who at the time was a Blessed. He also preached upon another mystic who had died within their own times, Mother Marie de Jesus (1797-1854) from the convent des Oiseaux of Paris who had received revelations from the Sacred Heart that were favourably recognised by the Archbishop of Paris. On June 21, 1823 the Sacred Heart revealed to Sr. Marie that He desired France be consecrated to His Sacred Heart by the King, and that a chapel be built and dedicated to Him, and the feast of the national consecration be formally celebrated every year. "After my sermon," recounts Fr. Boylesve, "the Mother Superior expressed to me her astonishment at my silence with regard to an almost similar order that Our Lord had given to Blessed Margaret Mary on June 17th, 1689. I confessed that in our college, which had barely opened for a month, I had not found the letters of the Blessed One and that I was unaware of the apparition and the order she was telling me about. I promised to make good this omission." Apparently at that time, the Sacred Heart's requests to St. Margaret Mary for a shrine and the national consecration of France by the King were not yet widely known.

True to his word, filled with his characteristic zeal for faith and country, doing what he could to extend the reign of Jesus Christ through his beloved homeland and secure its safety, the very next day he repaired his omission by publishing a pamphlet featuring the prophecies of St. Margaret Mary and Mother Marie de Jesus entitled "Triumph of France by the Sacred Heart", composing a special prayer of consecration to be said, which the Zouaves said every Friday as hope in the Sacred Heart was sorely needed. Paris was threatened with destruction by bombardments, then starvation by the invading Prussians, having commenced a siege around the city in September 1870. The siege continued until January 1871, the citizens reduced to dire circumstances. The zoo animals were slaughtered for food, the populace also living off of stray animals and rats. While the Prussian advance had ceased, humiliation still ensued when France suffered defeat at the hands of the Prussians with the establishment of the German Empire, also losing the territory of the Alsace-Lorraine to the victors. The troubles were not over. From March to May 1871 Paris fell into the clutches of the anticlerical socialist Communards, rebels revolting against the new government of the Third Republic. Blood ran in the streets, historical buildings burned, including the Tuileries Palace. The anticlerical Communards also executed the Archbishop of Paris, Georges Darboy, fulfilling the prophecy of St. Catherine Laboure. This horrific turn of events, combined with the circulation of prophecies foretelling the destruction of Paris was at hand, the faithful no doubt felt doom hung over the city. The times were desperate. After several reprintings, including a full reproduction of the text by Fr. Ramiere in the 'Messenger' newsletter issued by the Apostleship of Prayer, more than 330,000 copies of Fr. de Boylesve's pamphlets of the "Triumph of the Sacred Heart' were circulated. It contributed to the rapid spread devotion to the Sacred Heart and bolstered the call to have the Universal Church consecrated to the Sacred Heart, also to build a national shrine on Montmartre in atonement for the atrocities committed by the Communards who began their uprising there. Construction began in 1875, the cornerstone was laid on June 16, 1875, the day Bl. Pius IX encouraged all the faithful to pray the consecration to the Sacred Heart using the special formula composed by the Sacred Congregation of Rites for the 200th anniversary of the apparition of the Sacred Heart to St. Margaret Mary. The construction of Sacre Coeur was at last completed in 1914.

As for Fr. Boylesve, in addition to his efforts to spread devotion to the Sacred Heart he worked unceasingly at many other endeavours, not only as director of the Apostolate of Prayer in Le

Mans, but also with the Confraternities of Saint Joseph such as that of the Good Death, and also the Confraternity of the Agonizing Heart, the Work of Campaigns, Conferences of St. Vincent de Paul, Workers' Circles, he still appeared to dare all and sundry that they would never be able to find enough work for him to do. He amazed all that he was never at a loss for a subject to preach upon. He could easily vary his sermons to where it appeared he never preached the same way twice, and always captured his hearers' attention. One day out of curiosity a hardened sinner walked in to listen to him preach and left a converted man. When Fr. Boylesve wasn't working, he was praying. There was no question that he maintained a deep spiritual life. He was transferred to Vaugirard in 1875, returning to Le Mans two years later in 1877. Three years later his teaching came to an end at the college there with the decree of March 29, 1880 issued by the French minister for public education prohibiting the Jesuits from engaging in their educational apostolate, only the first of several anticlerical laws that would be passed in France over the next decades. Fr. Boylesve admitted he was on the verge of tears saying his last Mass for the students in the chapel before the school closed. Yet, he remained as active as ever despite this terrible blow, preaching, giving catechisms and continuing his writing, tackling the problems of their day threatening both the Church and society. He continued working despite his old age, until the end of 1891 when his activity was curtailed.

He was struck with various ailments, first a tormenting dermatitis that remained with him, then inflammation of the blood that restricted his activities for many weeks, although he managed to say Mass and continue his writing, until at last he was struck with paralysis, unable to walk or speak. Clutching his rosary and his crucifix, the ever zealous 'priest-knight' of the Vendée gave up his soul to God in February 22, 1892 and was buried in the Jesuit cemetery of Sainte-Croix.[1]

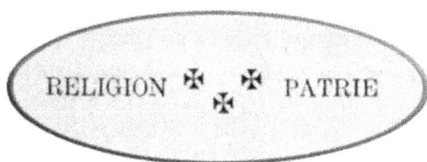

RELIGION ✠ ✠ PATRIE

---

1 Biographical information from 'Necrologie. Le Père Marin de Boyleseve, in 'Lettres de Jersey', Vol.XII, No. 1 (April 1893)

PREFACE

The most reliable foundation for the glory and veneration due to Saint Joseph is to be found within the pages of the Gospel. Thirty-three texts, comprising all that the New Testament narrative reveals concerning Saint Joseph, have been selected by us as the groundwork of a course of short practical Meditations inciting to the imitation of the virtues of the Saint, *as recorded in the Gospel.* These thirty-three chosen texts will teach the faithful how best to honour the great Patron of the Church, and the reasons for placing unlimited confidence in his protection.

This little manual contains a daily exercise for the Month of Saint Joseph; but devotion to this PATRON OF THE UNIVERSAL CHURCH should not be confined to one month, and as each Wednesday throughout the year has for a long time been dedicated to St. Joseph, a good way of carrying out this devotion might be to take for the subject of our Meditation some of the mysteries of the life of this great Saint as we find them recorded in the Gospel.

Of the three Feasts in honour of Saint Joseph, the chief one is that celebrated on the 19th of March. The second in order is that of the Patronage, fixed for the Third Sunday after Easter; and the third, common to Our Lady and her chaste Spouse falls on January 23rd and bears the name of Feast of the *Espousals of the Blessed Virgin and Saint Joseph.*

Three of the daily readings would form a Meditation for each day of the Novenas preceding these Feasts, and each Meditation might be concluded by the recitation of the prayers authorised to be used in honour of the Saint, and which will be found at the end of this little book, in company with other devotion to the august Spouse of the Mother of our Lord.

Fr. Marin de Boylesve, S.J.

SAINT JOSEPH,

ACCORDING TO THE GOSPEL

॰॰❀॰॰

1ˢᵗ Meditation

"And Jacob begot Joseph the husband of Mary, of whom was born Jesus, who is called the Christ." ~ SAINT MATTHEW i. 16.

Descendant of the kings of Judah, Spouse of the Mother of God, foster-father of Jesus, representative also of the Eternal Father, Joseph holds next to Mary the highest rank to which a mere creature can be exalted; and such a man passed unnoticed. No trait is cited, no word uttered that can win him a place in the annals of the world. He is named but in conjunction with Jesus and Mary, and that only so far as their interests require.

How vain all earthly glory! Much is said of those who desire oblivion, and true merit remains ignored.

Let the world despise us, its contempt

pass unheeded, and, far from feeling surprise, let us rejoice at being overlooked. The world has forgotten so many! We will repay oblivion by oblivion!

Watchword ~ *Heed neither the esteem nor the contempt of the world.*

Saint Joseph's Place in Heaven

An artist was commissioned by Pius IX to paint a picture of the proclamation of the Dogma of the Immaculate Conception. When the sketch was submitted for approval, the sovereign pontiff, looking at it exclaimed: "And Saint Joseph, where is he?" The artist pointed to a group lost in the clouds, replying: "This is the spot I reserve for him." "No, replied the Holy Father, pointing to a place at our Saviour's side; "there, and only there, must he be placed; for surely that is his post in heaven."

❧ ✿ ☙

2nd Meditation

"And in the sixth month, the Angel Gabriel was sent from God into a city of Galilee, called Nazareth, to a virgin espoused to a man whose name was Joseph, of the house of David: and the virgin's name was Mary." ~ SAINT LUKE i. 26, 27.

This son of David, the descendant of kings, is in the world's sight nought but a simple workman obliged to gain his bread by the sweat of his brow.

When God proposes working out some grand design, He renders lowly all the surroundings of the person whose greatness He intends to manifest. That masterpiece of the Divine Wisdom, Power and Love, the Incarnation, was to be divested of all earthly splendour; therefore, during three hundred years the house of David was lost sight of among the other families of Judah, Zerubbabel is the last king who plays any part in history. The branch to which Joseph belonged fell into indigence, and as there is nothing so efficacious as poverty to ensure the world's neglect, Joseph was in a fit position to be associated in the Divine work.

When God abases and humbles you, when He deprives you of the means of action, of the elements of success; when He appears to frustrate and annihilate your every effort, do not be alarmed. In this very way He is about to effect, by you and in you, some great work. Men despise, or worse still, they forget you and know you no more. This is the moment awaited by God. Now, will the Divine Power (such is the meaning of the name Gabriel) descend to visit you, and, as Mary and Joseph of old, so you too are about to be summoned to concur in the carrying on of the Divine work, in the development of the Incarnation, in the perfecting of the mysterious Body of Christ, in the extension of the Church, and the reign of Jesus.

Watchword ~ *Desire to be ignored, and to ignore oneself.*

Devotion to Saint Joseph _Counselled by Our Lady_

Father P. Balthazar Alvarez[2] being sick, a

---

2 Fr. Balthazar Alvarez (1534–1580) was a Spanish Catholic mystic and the spiritual director of St. Teresa of Avila.

religious presented him with an image of Saint Joseph, exhorting him to commend himself to the Holy Patriarch. "You are right," replied Father; "that is precisely what the Blessed Virgin counselled me to do." On hearing these words, a brother who had accompanied Father Alvarez in his journey to Rome, remembered that on quitting the Holy House of Loretto, the Father told him that he had just experienced a deep feeling of devotion to Saint Joseph. It is possible that was the moment when Our Lady exhorted the Father to confidence in her Holy Spouse.

಄⊛಄

3ʳᵈ Meditation

"When Mary was espoused to Joseph, before they came together, she was found with child of the Holy Ghost." ~ SAINT MATTHEW i. 18.

Mary was confided to Saint Joseph as a precious deposit. The mission of this just man was to shield the virginity of Mary. Meanwhile the work of the Holy Ghost is accomplished.

Let us simply observe our rule of life,

fulfil the duties of our calling, and God meanwhile will work out great things, accomplishing His designs, and inasmuch as we have been faithful to the mission entrusted to our care, God will associate us with Himself in the work that otherwise He would effect without our aid.

Joseph covers, so to speak, the Divine work; and thus God makes use of our words and example to give birth to Jesus in the hearts of men, whilst in reality it is His grace that effects these wonders.

Dignity of Saint Joseph

On the Feast of the Annunciation Saint Gertrude beheld in vision all the saints of heaven bend the head each time the choir uttered the name of Joseph; they exchanged glances, testifying their happiness at the glory Saint Joseph enjoys in heaven, and the honour rendered to him on earth.

జం❀ళ

4th Meditation

"Joseph her husband, being a just man, and not willing publicly to expose her, was minded to put her away privately." ~ SAINT MATTHEW i. 19.

The Holy Ghost proclaims Joseph a just man, and yet as being loth to accuse Mary; therefore the holy Patriarch must have been convinced of the perfect innocence of his angelic spouse, if not so, Joseph's resolve would have been contrary to the law and therefore to justice also.

Why, then, does Joseph meditate separation from Mary? It is doubtless that he deems himself unworthy of remaining with her in whom such mysteries were being enacted. What anxiety must not he have suffered in reconciling obedience to the law, with the respect due to the virtue of Mary? Admire the wisdom of this just man, who finds in withdrawing himself a way of conciliation.[*]

---

* Fr. Boylesve's meditation is in complete agreement with the interpretation of the Church Fathers and saints regarding the Gospel's description of St. Joseph as a just man, a man filled with virtue who fulfilled the Law of God. St. Jerome observes if St. Joseph had truly doubted Mary's innocence, he as a just man would have had to fulfil the Law of Moses in publicly denouncing her because the Law

However strong the external evidence against out neighbour ~ let us beware of judging him ~ I reflect what regret it would have caused Saint Joseph had he allowed himself to judge according to appearances.

Do you wish to spare yourself and your brethren sorrow ~ too often irreparable ~ judge not your neighbour, speak not and act not against his interests, save in case of publicity, of certainty, or of necessity.

---

did not allow for any concealment of sin in this matter, to conceal such a sin was to be a partaker in it, and St. Joseph could not be described 'just' if he broke the Law.   However as he did not denounce her, St. Joseph was fully convinced of her sinless innocence and that Our Lady had conceived by the power of God.   Why then did he resolve to separate himself from her and put her away privately if she was innocent?   The Angel's words to him give the answer: 'Son of David, fear not to take unto thee Mary thy wife.' (Matt. 1:20) The Church Fathers have concluded St. Joseph felt a holy fear and deemed himself unworthy to take the Mother of the Saviour and the Son of God under his roof, and therefore resolved to put her away quietly.   Therefore as a just man he could not condemn her under the Law of Moses, and in his deep humility, was convinced he was unworthy to be near her.   As the Gospel shows, the Angel comforted him and revealed he too, a son of David, was part of God's great plan to care for the Mother of God and be the foster father of the Saviour, also to have the great honour of giving Him His name as His father.   See the chapter 'Joseph's Trial' in 'The Glories of St. Joseph', by Edward Healy Thompson, M.A., (Burnes and Oates, London, 1888), pp. 192-202.

Watchword ~ *Judge not, and you shall not be judged.*

Saint Joseph and the Two Professors[+]

During the time that Father Lallemand[3] was rector of the college at Bourges, as the Feast of Saint Joseph drew near the Rev. Father sent for two young professors, and promised to obtain for them any grace they desired, provided that they would exhort their pupils to devotion towards Saint Joseph. The two religious gladly consented to the proposal, and their efforts were so successful that on the day of the Feast all their pupils received holy Communion. The same day the two professors went to the rector, and each of them privately named the grace he desired. The first, the

---

[+]   Fr. Boylesve did not mention Fr. Lallemand also had the two professors say a Nine Day Novena to St. Joseph of his own invention called the 'Four Visits' Novena. See the Appendix on the 'Four Visits' Novena and how to say it.

3   Fr. Louis Lallemand (1588-1635), Jesuit priest and French theologian, noted for sanctity and as a master of the spiritual life. He is the author of the first important treatise or synthesis of Ignatian spirituality, which was written between 1620 and 1630. He was for a few months before his death the rector of College Sainte-Marie de Bourges.

eminent Father Nouet,[4] entreated the privilege of speaking and writing worthily of our Saviour. We do not know the favour desired by the other, we only know that it was obtained. As for Father Nouet, he, on the morrow of the Feast, returned to the rector, saying that he had changed his mind, as on reflection, he thought it his duty to ask for some grace more necessary to his own perfection. The rector replied that it was too late now, for Saint Joseph had already granted the favour at first requested.[5]

---

4   Possibly the French Jesuit and theologian. Fr. Jacques Nouet who was born in Mayenne March 25, 1605 and died in Paris May 21, 1680. He is noted for his writings against the Jansenist heresy. He also wrote against the Protestants and defended the Real Presence of Jesus in the Blessed Sacrament, and was one of the influences that contributed to the conversion of the Protestant Viscomte of Turenne, Henri de La Tour d'Auvergne, to Catholicism in 1668. The Viscomte became Marshal of France in 1643 and General Marshal of the King's camps and armies in 1660. He was one of the most distinguished generals of Kings Louis XIII and Louis XIV.

5   Difficult to know what Fr. Boylesve meant by giving this example, other than St. Joseph was pleased the professors followed the request to say the 'Four Visits' Novena, and spread devotion to him with great success. As a reward St. Joseph granted their requests so quickly that it was not possible to change the grace they desired of him!

Fr. Nouet obviously received his request to have the grace to write eloquently if he helped to convert the Viscomte of Turenne, see the footnote above.

5th Meditation

"While Joseph thought on these things, behold the Angel of the Lord appeared to him in his sleep." ~ SAINT MATTHEW i. 20

What honour for Saint Joseph thus to be deemed worthy of retaining her as spouse, who, by the operation of the Holy Ghost, had become the Mothcr of God!

We must admit that he had by this prudence and discretion proved himself worthy of the high mission entrusted to him. In similar circumstances how many would by their precipitation have ruined all! Joseph is lord of his own mind and heart. He takes time to reflect: *Hæc autem eo cogitant.*

Let us think before we act, think before we speak, think even before pronouncing interiorly, especially when our neighbour's honour is concerned. Let us wait for light from above, and when we have used all possible means and applied all the resources of our mind and will, suddenly, and at the very moment when we least expect it, God will send His angel: *"Hæc autem eo cogitante, ecce angelus Domini apparuit in sominis ei."*

During sleep, in the hours of the night, at the moment when we end our research, or at the moment when all is dark around, light will appear, inspiration will arrive, and the Divine Will be declared.

Watchword ~ _Reflect before you speak or act._

Patronage of Saint Joseph

Saint Teresa relates that at the Feast of the Assumption Saint Joseph appeared and covered her with a mantle of brilliant whiteness, revealing to her at the same time that she was justified from all her sins, and that he would obtain for her all the favour she desired.

Saint Teresa had dedicated the greater part of her convents to Saint Joseph, but after her decease some of these houses were placed under her protection. The saint appeared to one of the religious and gave her this strict order: Tell the Father Provincial to remove my name from the houses and restore them that of Saint Joseph.

The Dream of St. Joseph

6th Meditation

"Joseph, son of David, fear not to take unto thee Mary thy wife, for that which is conceived in her is of the Holy Ghost." ~ SAINT MATTHEW i. 20.

Son of David, descendant of the Prophet-King; of him who in vision beheld the eternal reign of the Messiah. Joseph, let the recollection of thy origin recall to thee the wondrous thing that shall be effected in thy line! The prediction of thy ancestor is about to be accomplished in the womb of the Virgin of Jesse, co-descendant with thee of the line of David, the Holy Virgin whose fate is linked with thine! Fear not, thou son of David, to remain with thy spouse, Virgin Daughter of David's royal line! Thou art worthy of her, and to thee is confided that sacred deposit, the divine treasure of her virginity! True, it is by the operation of the Holy Ghost that she has become a mother, but she ceases not to be thy spouse. She and her Son are thine! An orphan here below, the Son of the Most High, and Mary's Son needs an earthly father, this father thou shalt be, for it is thy right: *Noli timere accipere Mariam conjugem tuam.*

Is anxiety at its climax, difficulty insuperable, do thou thy best. Reflect, seek for a way to extricate thyself and then resolve: *Hæc autem eo cogitante*; but act with calmness like Joseph in spite of anxiety, sleep thou in peace in the arms of a living Providence. The night of trial shall usher in a brilliant day. You fell asleep in sorrow, you shall awake in joy!

<u>Watchword</u> ~ *Hope ever; God is faithful.*

<u>Saint Joseph and Saint Ignatius</u>

Saint Ignatius, founder of the Society of Jesus, was ever mindful of Saint Joseph. In his "Exercises" he proposes the Saint to our consideration in relation to our Lord's hidden life. In his oratory was an image of Saint Joseph, before which he loved to pray, and when any extraordinary difficulty occurred, it was on this spot that Saint Ignatius put it into writing, in order to obtain a happy solution.

❦ ❦ ❦

7th **Meditation**

"Mary shall bring forth a son; and thou shalt call His name Jesus, for He shall save His people from their sins."
~ SAINT MATTHEW i. 21.

Now Joseph comprehends the high degree of honour to which union with Mary admits him. He is chosen as father to Mary's Son, the Son of God, and the honour will be his of bestowing on the Divine Child the admirable name of JESUS, a name which in itself designates all that He is, and all that He will be!

No longer let us murmur at Joseph's silence. We know but one word that issued from his lips, but by this one word Joseph has revealed more than all the Prophets of the Old, and as much as the Apostles and Doctors of the New Testament: for Joseph has named JESUS.

The prophets foretold what Messiahs would do and say, but none declared His name; but this name in itself reveals all that Jesus is, all that Jesus will be. The Apostles can tell us no more than this. If they traverse the world, it is to preach the name of Jesus; if they create astonishment by their miracles, it is because they work them in the name of Jesus; whether they suffer, whether they die, it is for the name of Jesus.

The Doctors speak and write but to explain, propagate, and defend the Faith in the name of Jesus; and Saint Bernard exclaims, as did Saint Paul, the he knows but one thing, but one word ~ Jesus. All the Doctors and all the Apostles say the same.

For ourselves, let there be fewer words, fewer ideas. One suffices. With Joseph let us seek but Jesus, think but Jesus, speak but Jesus, serve but Jesus, act but for Jesus, and then shall we never be separated from Jesus.

Watchword ~ *Invoke incessantly the Holy Name of Jesus.*

The Three Great Names

Father Gaspard Bon[6] began and ended all his questions, and all his replies by invoking the holy names of Jesus, Mary and Joseph, and expired uttering these sacred

---

6 Bl. Gasper Bon, also known as Bl. Gaspar de Bono (1530 -1604) was a Spanish friar of the Order of Minims.

names, which are in themselves a pledge of salvation.

❧ ✿ ❧

8th Meditation

"And Joseph, rising up from sleep, did as the Angel of the Lord had commanded him, and took unto him his wife." ~ SAINT MATTHEW i. 24.

Here two things in the conduct of Joseph strike me forcibly ~ its simplicity and its promptitude. The Angel has spoken: instantly, without question or hesitation, Joseph obeys: *Fecit sicut præcepit.* Admirable simplicity! How this straightforwardness bears away the palm from human prudence, with its many calculations ~ its sinuosities and its deliberations. True, it is permissible to hesitate, and as already said, we must suspend our judgement and reflect carefully when we are in doubt: *Hæc eo cogitante*; but when once God has spoken, whether by the voice of Angel or of man, by a ray of human intelligence or a feeling of the heart, arise and act: *Ex surgens fecit sicut præcepit.* In the hour of anguish let silence be our wisdom, and the voice of God our light; suddenly the darkness shall be dispelled ~ all obstacles will disappear; our desires and our designs will be realised, and that far beyond our fondest expectations.

Watchword ~ *What it is your duty to do, do it resolutely, promptly, and simply.*

Saint Joseph and Saint Francis de Sales

Saint Francis de Sales being at Lyons on the Feast of Saint Joseph, preached at the Carmelites. As soon as the sermon was ended, the Superior of the Jesuits came to the Saint and entreated him to preach at their church, dedicated to Saint Joseph. "I confess," replied the amiable Prelate, "that two sermons a day are rather beyond my powers; still, for love of Saint Joseph, I will do my best." He did so, and it was well seen that Saint Joseph was his saint of predilection. The Superior was about to thank him when the Prelate exclaimed: "But, Father, do you not perceive how entirely I am devoted to Saint Joseph?"

This same Father being with the good

Bishop one day previous to his death, asked permission to make use of his breviary, and remarked that in it there was but one picture, that of Saint Joseph.

ॐ

9th Meditation

"And Joseph knew not Mary till she had brought forth her first-born Son, and he called His name Jesus." ~ SAINT MATTHEW i. 25.

Jesus is called first-born of Mary, because at the foot of the Cross the Immaculate Virgin was to become the Mother of the human race ~ these represented in the person of St. John. Joseph and Mary led the life of angels, and towards the Divine Child Saint Joseph exercised all the rights and fulfilled all the duties and offices of father.

In the first place, it is he who has the honour of naming Mary's Son ~ an honour we have said that exalts Joseph far above Patriarchs, Apostles, and Doctors. Now, if the name of Jesus is the only word that we have from the lips of Joseph, this single word reveals the one thought which filled the mind, heart, and life of Saint Joseph.

Great Saint, obtain for me this one favour ~ to know Jesus, and to know but Jesus. I shall do this, if Jesus, and Jesus alone, is first in my mind and heart, on my lips and in my hands, that is to say, first in my thoughts and my affections, in my words and in my actions. May it be my one ambition, my sole happiness and glory to study Jesus and His Gospel, to serve Jesus and His Church!

Watchword ~ *You are a Christian: be proud of this name.*

Joseph and the Infant Jesus

Yolande of Silva, of the Order of Saint Dominic, had an especial veneration for Saint Joseph, because he had the happiness of hearing the cries of the Infant JESUS, of beholding Him during the days of His infancy, of carrying Him, of caressing and fondling Him with loving reverence.

10ᵗʰ **Meditation**

"And it came to pass that in those days there went out a decree from Caesar Augustus, that the whole world should be enrolled. And all went to be enrolled, every one into his own city."
~ *SAINT LUKE ii. 1,3.*

Joseph, in virtue of his royal descent should have commanded, he obeys; his heritage was a throne, and yet among the lowly is his home!

True greatness and liberty are independent of social position. Many a one appears to hold a higher rank than his brethren, and is in reality but the puppet of those whom in semblance and fancy he commands. He ranks as first, and is but last and lowest of all. In the most holy position one may be as great, as free, as ever was monarch on his throne!

In the sight of God and of the angels, Joseph fills the highest and most regal position in the world. Augustus governs Rome, and through Rome the world. Joseph rules but one family, commands but two subjects; but this family is comprised of Jesus and Mary ~ Mary, the Mother of Jesus, and Jesus, God and King over all the Cæsars and nations of the world!

Do you aspire to be great and free? To possess real authority and lasting influence over men? Humble yourself and obey. God and man resists the proud. Give way to others and cede in all things where truth and justice demand not the contrary. Thus and thus only will you be found strong and free when called on to defend the interests of God and of your neighbour.

Saint Joseph's Power Revealed by Our Lady

"My daughter," said the Blessed Virgin to one of her faithful clients, "words fail to reveal the eminent sanctity of Saint Joseph. Only in heaven will this deep and admirable mystery be fathomed. At the Judgement Day numbers of the lost will bitterly lament having slighted and neglected so powerful a protector. The world ignores the greatness of the prerogatives bestowed by God on my holy spouse. Seek his intercession in every hour of need, and strive to augment the number of his clients.[7]   God grants on earth all that my spouse demands in heaven."

❧ ✤ ☙

11th Meditation

"And Joseph went up from Galilee out of the city of Nazareth into Judea, to the city of David, which is called Bethlehem, because he was of the house and family of David." ~ SAINT LUKE ii. 4.

The journey was trying to Mary, and hardly less so to Saint Joseph, to whom fall all the anxiety and fatigue of seeking a shelter, and to whom all the humiliating refusals were addressed. Bethlehem is David's city, but no shelter will David's son find there for David's daughter, Mary, Mother of the King of kings! Not a murmur is uttered, no cloud o'ershadows the peace of Joseph's soul or the even serenity of his brow.

We can readily picture the smile with which Joseph's utterance is received when he claims to be enrolled as a descendant of the

---

7   I.e. increase the number of those devoted to him.

house of David! If Caesar has aught to fear, the danger will not proceed from this scion of Judah's royal line!

And yet, who at this moment reigns in Rome, and from Rome sways the world? Where is Caesar? Vanished, together with his empire, in order to give place to the Vicegerent of Him whom Bethlehem rejected, and whom one of Caesar's servants inscribed among the lowliest of his master's subjects. Let us beware of judging according to outward appearance, or we too might have despised Joseph, the spouse of Mary, of Mary, Mothcr of Jesus, King of kings. Eternal Word ~ very God and very man.

Let us not blush to appear poor and lowly; the world metes out its esteem and its contempt according to outward semblance; it falls prostrate at the feet of a poor miserable wretch, provided he wears a crown, and disdains true greatness, if greatness wears the livery of the poor.

We say again, and cannot too often reiterate: despise the world's contempt; more, if possible, than its esteem and honours; then and only then will you possess true liberty, and only then will you be truly great.

<u>Watchword</u> ~ *Appear less than you really are.*

<u>The Venerable de la Salle and Saint Joseph</u>

The Venerable de la Salle[8] placed his institution under the patronage of Saint Joseph, and daily recited the litanies of the Saint, recommending his brethren to do so likewise in order that Saint Joseph's tender care of the Infant Jesus might serve as a model to them in bringing up the children entrusted to their care. The Saint proved how dear the Venerable Father was to his heart; when he fell sick, his strength returned on the eve of Saint Joseph's Day, and he was able to say Mass, his last, on the morning of the Feast. His health appeared to have been given back but for that purpose, for he soon experienced a relapse, and, in a few days, fell asleep in the Lord.

❧ ✿ ❧

---

8   St. Jean-Baptise de la Salle (1651-1719).

12th Meditation

"And they found Mary and Joseph, and the Infant Jesus lying in a manger." ~ SAINT LUKE 11. 16.

Contemplate Saint Joseph at the foot of the Crib. How unspeakable his bliss! The Divine Child gazes smilingly at him, and one such look suffices to obliterate all anxiety.

For Joseph, the past and future are effaced; he lives but in the present and enjoys celestial peace. So in our lives there are times of extraordinary peace and joy and the soul listens, breathes, enjoys, and possesses happiness in a manner so spiritual as to be inexpressible by human tongue.

Such was the happiness of Saint Joseph in the presence of the new-born Jesus. He adores in silence and his silence is one of awe. Is this the Word by Whom all things were created? By Whom all things subsist? ~ Silence of admiration! The Word is made Flesh, and we have beheld His glory! His birth reveals His love; angels have sung His greatness; the star announces His power; and ere long His word will reveal His wisdom and His deed show forth His might. ~ Silence of joy!

This stable, this crib, contain Him Who is the glory of Heaven and of the heavenly hosts. ~ Silence of grief! He has come to His own, and His own have received Him not. For the Son of David, for the Son of God, no place is found in Bethlehem!

The heart needs but Jesus. In Him are all treasures, joys, and honours.

Look at Mary and Joseph. Around them is nought but poverty, suffering, and humiliation. What matter? They are happy: Jesus is there!

Watchword ~ *In thought and affection live with Jesus.*

Feast of Saint Joseph in Canada

On the Eve of Saint Joseph, 1637,[9] the French flag was hoisted in Quebec, amid the roar of cannon. The salutes of fireworks so astonished the natives that they exclaimed: "Saint Joseph must indeed be a very great personage, for in his honour night is turned to day!" On the morrow the churches were crowded, as at Easter, and every one blessed God for having given, as patron to New France, that chosen one who during life was the protector and adopted father of the Incarnate Word.

---

9   Devotion to St. Joseph was particularly strong with the Missionaries sent to Canada. He was chosen as the patron saint of Canada by the first Recollect Franciscan missionaries in 1624. The Jesuit missionaries who followed the Franciscans dedicated and named several of their missions to St. Joseph. Many of the native Huron converts also took the name of St. Joseph after their baptism. St. Joseph's feast day was celebrated in Quebec by the early settlers with displays of fireworks, bonfires, and holy Benediction. Pope Urban VIII confirmed St. Joseph as Canada's patron in 1637 ~ the celebrations were very festive that year as we can see from Fr. Boylesve's description.

13th Meditation

"And after the days of her purification according to the law of Moses were accomplished, they carried him to Jerusalem, to present him to the Lord." ~ SAINT LUKE ii. 22.

Here we have proof of Joseph's legal right over the Son of Mary. With Mary he shares the merit and honour of presenting the Infant Jesus to the Eternal Father.

True, Jesus has no other Father than the One of Whom He will so often speak as "My Heavenly Father," or simply "My Father"; and yet Jesus belongs to Joseph. He who possesses the tree has a right to the fruit. The rights of Joseph over Mary ensure him equal rights over Jesus, and the Gospel shows us Joseph and Mary acting in concert, and both presenting the Infant Jesus. They carried Him: *tulerunt*; they presented Him: ut *sisterent*. It is not undesignedly that the sacred historian here employs the plural.

Let us learn to make good use of God's gifts. Joseph is associated with Mary in her rights over Jesus. Jesus belongs to Joseph even as He belongs to Mary. Like Mary and with Mary Joseph offers to God that which he has received from God. "According to the law:" *secundum legem Moysi*...Now, not only the law of Moses, but the law of nature, the law of gratitude, and, I must add, the law of our own self-interest, all teach us the solemn obligation we are under of rendering God homage for the gifts received from Him.

Intelligence, will, health, strength, eye, ear, tongue, hand, soul and body, life, fortune, power, are all so many gifts, to be consecrated to the glory and service of God, of Him who is so liberal in the gifts bestowed on you now, and the glory with which He will reward the generosity of your offering.

Watchword ~ *Offer to God all you are, all that you have.*

Saint Joseph and France in the Seventeenth Century

In 1661 Louis XIV, at the urgent entreaty of two queens, expressed by letters royal his desire that the Feast of Saint Joseph should be declared a Day of Obligation. The Bishop by their mandates, and the High Courts by their decrees, deferred to the royal wish, which was carried out in the 19th of March of the same year. Bossuet[10] preached his second panegyric on Saint Joseph, and ended it by thanking the King for his desire to render increased honour to the memory of the Saint.[11]

---

10 Bishop Jacques-Bénigne Bossuet (1627-1704). See the footnotes for the 14th Meditation.

11 This is in reference to the apparition of St. Joseph on June 7, 1660 in the south-eastern town of Cotignac, France. During a scorching hot day a shepherd named Gaspard Ricard sheltered under the trees near Mt. Bessillon and was tormented with thirst. A dignified man appeared, pointed to a rock and said "I am Joseph. Lift this rock and you shall drink." The rock was large and Gaspard did not think he could lift it, but the man insisted. The shepherd could lift it easily and water gushed forth. After quenching his thirst, he turned to thank the man, but he was gone. Gaspard ran to the village and told everyone. He was mocked until people went to the spot, saw the spring and tried to move the rock, which took eight men to lift! Word spread and miracles happened as people made pilgrimages to the site. King Louis XIV heard about the apparition and the miracles, which impressed him greatly. He consecrated

14th Meditation

"And to offer a sacrifice according as it is written in the law of the Lord, a pair of turtle doves, or two young pigeons." ~ SAINT LUKE ii. 24.

Descendant of the kings of Judah, Joseph is reduced to the offering of the poor; but this causes him no shame, he esteems himself richer than the richest kings, richer than even David or Solomon in all their glory, for Joseph possesses Jesus. Though poor in this world's goods he see no disgrace in that. For himself, is not he the spouse of Mary and the adopted Father of Jesus? And Mary? She is the Mother of Jesus. And the Child? That very Son of David, whose reign shall know no limit, no end, and whose throne shall be eternal!

What is there humiliating in poverty or glorious in riches? If I am poor it is either because I will it or God wills it, and this consciousness frees me from the fetters which

all France to St. Joseph on March 19, 1661 and declared the Feast of St. Joseph a national holiday throughout the kingdom.

turn man into a slave to gold. Shall I then blush at a poverty that assures me independence, liberty, nobility, and grandeur! No, it shall not be this. I will desire not only to be but to appear poor, for I wish to be like Jesus, Mary, and Joseph.

Watchword *~Let your requirements be less each day.*

Saint Joseph and Bossuet

In 1657 Bossuet[12] preached in Saint Joseph's honour a sermon so beautiful that he was called on to repeat it two years later in the presence of the Queen-mother. It was that the sermon which has for text: *'Depositum custodi.* On the 19th of March 1661 Anne of Austria desired again to listen to the great orator, who, applying to Saint Joseph the

12 Bishop Jacques-Bénigne Bossuet (1627-1704) was a French bishop, theologian and Court Preacher to Louis XIV of France famed for his sermons and public addresses. He was considered to be the most brilliant public orators of all time and a master French stylist. He was particularly devoted to St. Joseph. See the 13th Meditation. It is possible to find copies of his sermons, including 'Depositum custodi' mentioned above by Fr. Boylesve.

words addresses to David when Samuel came to anoint him king of Israel, preached from this text: *Quæsivit sibi Deus virum juxta cor suum* ~ "God has sought for Himself a man after His own heart."

❧ ✿ ❧

15th Meditation

"And when His parents brought in the child Jesus, to do for Him according to the custom of the law." ~ SAINT LUKE 11. 27

His parents: *Parentes ejus.* Thus again does the Holy Ghost plainly recognise and indicate Saint Joseph as the adopted father of Jesus. What has he done to merit so signal a share in the work of the world's redemption? It is hinted at in the Presentation. Many fancy that rank dispenses from the observance of the ordinary precept of life, and greatness consists in imagining oneself superior to all rule. Joseph thinks otherwise.

The Presentation in the Temple

Here is a law that concerns not the Holy Trinity, for what purification can she need, who, as Virgin-Mother, sanctifies by her mere presence? What stain can she have contracted in conceiving in her chaste womb and in giving birth to the Holy One: *Quod nascetur ex te sanctum*. Joseph and Mary know but one law, and on the day appointed they present themselves in the temple to take part in a ceremony which, in the eyes of man, associates Mary with the ordinary mothers of the human race.

Prudence and dignity consists first of all in the simple, regular, and faithful observance of the commandments of God and of the Church, of the rules of our profession, and the duties of our state. Law rule, such is the expression of God's will concerning us; and all our wisdom and all our virtue consists in conforming our intelligence and will to the Divine wisdom and goodness as manifested in the Law.

<u>Watchword</u> ~ *Live up to your rule, and you will live to God.*

Growth of Devotion to Saint Joseph

In the brief which Pius IX raised the Association of the Children of Saint Joseph into an Arch-Confraternity, the holy Father speaks this: "There is nothing we desire so much as to see a daily increase of devotion to Saint Joseph, spouse of the Blessed Virgin."

A learned and pious religious of the sixteenth century, who, on the testimony of Benedict XIV, has written a most remarkable work on St. Joseph, in his _Somme_ expresses himself thus with regard to the gifts bestowed on Saint Joseph: ~

"In Eastern countries the Holy Ghost has filled men's hearts with the desire of rendering great honour to Saint Joseph; and we are sure that this devotion will obtain for us, by the merits and intercession of this glorious Patriarch, the withdrawal of many danger by which the Church is assailed, and for the faithful an abundance of grace."

❧ ✿ ❧

16th Meditation

"And His father and mother were wondering at these things which were spoken concerning Him." ~ SAINT LUKE ii. 33.

Yet again once more does the Holy Ghost recognise and indicate Saint Joseph as the adopted father of Jesus. Whence arises the surprise felt by Joseph and Mary at that which is spoken concerning Jesus? Is it because of the great things foretold by Simeon and by Anna? No; they know that Jesus is indeed the Great One: *Hic erit magnus*; and when, in obeying God's command, they gave Him the name of Jesus, they knew that it was a name above all names. That which now seems to cause them wonder is beholding the hidden greatness of the Divine Child acknowledged and revealed by others. They admire and rejoice at the honour that accrues to Jesus.

Let us not envy those who have the happiness to glorify God in a higher degree than ourselves. If you love Jesus and seek His glory, so that He is loved and glorified, whether by your efforts and your labours or by those of others, your joy will be the same.

It is not always those who serve Jesus most openly by word or pen who contribute most to His service and glory. Who dare assert that Simeon or Anna had done more for the glory of Jesus than did Mary? Or that Prophets, Apostles, Martyrs, and Doctors have done and suffered more for Jesus than did His Blessed Mother?

You cannot sever the action of Joseph from that of Mary, for Joseph shared all the anxieties and care of his spouse; he it is who nurtured, protected, guided, and tended both the Mother and the Child.

Let us be content to leave brilliant words and deeds to those whom the Holy Ghost inspires. By your incessant desires, your upright, simple, and pure intention, doing God's will in your respective spheres; one in the world and amid the embarrassment[13] of business or of a family: another in the solitude of the cloister, unknown to man and even to those by whom he is surrounded, feeling that what you are and what you do is of but little value, you may contribute to the glory of Jesus and much, and often more, than missionaries, bishops, preachers, doctors, and than Popes most eminent in word and deed.

_____

13 i.e. difficulties.

Watchword ~ *Seek glory, but let it be the glory of Jesus.*

Alms in Honour of Saint Joseph

The community of La Miséricorde,[14] at Laval, found it necessary to erect some buildings, but funds were wanting. It was the month of March 1844. A Novena was made in honour of Saint Joseph, and a few days after the Superior of the Community, Mother Theresa, received from a lady at Rennes the sum of 7000 francs. The gift was accompanied by a letter stating that the idea of making the offering had entered her mind on Saint Joseph's Day.

ॐ ✿ ॐ

---

14 Fr. Boylesve is referring to the order Les Soeurs de Notre-Dame de Miséricorde (Sisters of Our Lady of Mercy) founded by Therese Rondeau (1793-1866).

17th Meditation

"And after they had performed all things according to the law of the Lord, they returned into Galilee, into their city Nazareth." ~ Saint Luke ii. 39.

Joseph and Mary leave their home only to accomplish the precept of the law; that duty fulfilled, they return to their solitude.

Let us also love the calm and tranquillity of a retired life, and only appear in the world when duty or charity demand; but when summoned by duty let us accomplish with exactitude and fidelity all that charity, the glory of God, and the good of our neighbour require. So Mary and Joseph return to Nazareth, only when they have fully accomplished all that the law demanded: *Et ut perficerent omnia secundum legem Domini.* When we have effected any good, we are sometimes tempted to cling to the work that has succeeded so well, and to the persons whom we have benefited. Let us reject this illusion and escape from the praise and thanks of men. Return to our hidden life, court oblivion, and remain in our retirement until called to quit it by the manifestation of the Divine will or the necessities of our neighbour.

Watchword ~ _To do good, and to annihilate self._

The Little Sisters of the Poor and Saint Joseph

The Little Sisters of the Poor at Roanne owed 2000 francs. The time of payment was at hand, and the cash-box was still empty. True, they daily found sufficient food for their poor, but 2000 francs were not so easy to find. "Saint Joseph alone can rescue us," said the Sisters; "let us commence a Novena." They do so and deposit their request at the foot of the statue of their patron. Before the close of the Novena, the Superioress was sent for by a stranger who had been taken ill at the hotel. "Sister," said the lady, "have you a chamber to spare for me?" ~ "Madame," replied the sister, "we receive only poor old men; but I can tell you of a house that will suit you much better than would ours." ~ "Sister," replied the stranger, "I suppose you do not refuse alms?" ~ "They are our only resource," answered the Superioress. The lady then took a purse and presented it to the sister, who, on opening it, was overwhelmed with gratitude to find that it contained just the 2000 francs for which they had petitioned Saint Joseph.

❧ ✿ ☙

18th Meditation

"Behold the Angel of the Lord appeared in sleep to Joseph, saying: Arise and take the Child and His Mother, and fly into Egypt; and be there until I shall tell thee: For it will come to pass that Herod will seek the Child to destroy Him." ~ SAINT MATTHEW ii. 13

But this is a dream! And on the faith of a nocturnal vision which may prove to be only a delusion, will it be wise to heed the warning and take so strange a course?

This Child is God! And must He have recourse to flight to escape a tyrant's rage?

The vengeance[15] of the angel's message renders the exile yet more appalling: *Et esto ibi usque dum dicam tibi* ~ remain in Egypt until I tell thee to return.

But if this vision be indeed from heaven, what a responsibility even then! At this very moment, perchance the tyrant's emissaries are at hand ready to slay the Infant at His Mother's breast.

---

15 I.e. the gravity of the angel's message.

What step must be taken?   Shall he regard the vision as but an idle dream, or at once incur the danger of a hasty flight?

Joseph is as superior to human reasonings as he is to trouble and alarm. In him faith is predominant; but where shall I seek this calmness, so simple and sublime, free from the hesitation of doubt, unmoved by the storm of passion?

Be attentive and obedient to the inspiration with which grace constantly presents[*] us, then shall we easily discern the true from the false, and neither be misled by vain reasoning nor by the fears of a restless mind.

Watchword ~ *Calmly obey the voice of Divine inspiration.*

---

[*] Original translation had 'prevents'. Could be a typo and 'presents us' was actually intended.

The Lucky Number

A young man was about to draw for the conscription.[16] On his way he entered a chapel dedicated to Saint Joseph ~ *des Champs*, near Laval. "You know," said he to the Saint: "how I dread military service; less on account of the hardships and dangers of war than because of the idleness and immorality of the barracks. Here is the number which I desire." Saying this he placed the number on the altar and went his way. At the moment of putting his hand into the urn he invoked Saint Joseph, and withdrew the very number he had named. He hastened to the sanctuary and returned heartfelt thanks to the Saint.

❧ ✿ ❧

---

16   When conscription was introduced in France every man aged 20 years or older had to enlist, but it was decided through the means of drawing lots who had to undertake service in the army. This story shows St. Joseph gave the man the lot number he requested and therefore was saved from occasions of sin in the immoral environment of the army barracks.

19ᵗʰ Meditation

"Joseph arose, and took the Child and His Mother by night, and retired into Egypt." ~ Saint Matthew ii. 14.

Admire the promptitude and calmness of this act of obedience: *Qui consurgens*. The Angel has spoken, Joseph arises. He commands in as straightforward and simple a manner as he obeys ~ he uses no subterfuge with regard to many, but takes the Infant and His Mother: *Accepit puerum et matrem ejus* ~ and at once they set forth. *Nocte*: that very night, without objection, hesitation, or delay, the command of heaven is obeyed.

The world is surprised at the activity of the Saints, at the multiplicity of their works. Let us reflect on the time we lose in resisting the Divine inspiration, the orders of Providence, the claims of duty, and the rights of obedience. If we simply do what God wills, we shall find time for all.

Remark the parallel in the words of the Angel and the conduct of Joseph. The acts of the latter respond word for word to the commands of the former. The Angel has spoken: "Arise," *Surge*, and Joseph arises: *Qui consurgens*. "Take the Child and His Mother," adds the Celestial Messenger, and Joseph takes the Child and His Mother. *Accipe puerum et matrem ejus*; ~ *Accepit puerum et matrem ejus*. Again the Angel continues: Flee into Egypt, and Joseph flees into Egypt. *Fuge in Ægyptum; ~ Secessit in Ægyptum.*

Let the rule of your conduct be the Word of God, whether manifest by the voice of those whom He has given you as Superiors, in the Church, in the family, in your own special sphere, in the rules of your profession, in the inspirations of grace, and the external leadings of Providence, and then your walk will be sure and firm, calm and rapid: all difficulties will vanish, all obstacles disappear.

Behold Saint Joseph, *Secessit in Ægyptum*, he retires in Egypt. The words are so short and simple that at first we dread, not of the anxiety, pain, and peril of so long and sudden a journey. But God has spoken, God wills it, therefore nothing is difficult, nothing impossible.

__Watchword__ ~ *Before obedience all difficulties vanish.*

The Shipwreck and the Seven Paters and Aves

Two Franciscans who had been shipwrecked were clinging to a fragment of timber, where for three days they remained between life and death. At last they recommended themselves to Saint Joseph, and at once a majestic youth appeared and steered them to shore. On landing, the two religious threw themselves at the feet of their liberator, entreating him to reveal his name. "I am Joseph, whom you invoked," replied he: "and if you wish to give me pleasure, let no day pass without reciting seven Paters and Aves in memory of the seven joys and seven dolours of my earthly life." That said, he disappeared, leaving the two religious overwhelmed by gratitude and joy.[17]

&❀&

17　　This happened off the coast of Flanders. For the Seven Sorrows and Joys of St. Joseph, see the Appendix.

20th Meditation

"And Joseph remained in Egypt until the death of Herod." ~ SAINT MATTHEW ii. 15.

Another of those words which indicate more than appears at first sight. He was there: *Erat ibi*; but what was his position and how did he live? Picture to yourself a poor artisan all at once transported to a foreign land where he knows no one, is known of none, is without means, tools, work, or home. Ah! What are the anxieties and inconveniences of Bethlehem compared with the cares and sufferings of Egypt? At Bethlehem they at least knew the extent of their sojourn, it was but for a few days, but of their stay in Egypt they know nought, neither can they even conjecture the duration of their exile.

"Remain there," said the Angel, "until I return." In face of a future so uncertain it is vain to think of any permanent abode; and yet, with all the inconveniences inseparable from a temporary sojourn, that sojourn will last for years.

Who can tell the sadness experienced by

the Holy Family at sight of the idolatry of Egypt? In presence of this sorrow all the privations of exile grow pale and vanish. God ignored, God offended, souls lost, ah! What grief to the heart of Jesus, and therefore to the hearts of Mary and Joseph also!

The Holy Family in Egypt is a type of the Church in the world. The Church is there: the Pope is there: *Et erat ibi*, always threatened by Herod and awaiting the tyrant's death: *Usque ad obitum Herodis.*

Such, too, is the situation of those persons and societies who dedicate themselves to God's service. In the ages of faith they built for the future; but now times are changed. A work is commenced, and to-morrow the breath of Revolution or a tyrant's caprice stays your projects or destroys your undertaking. Labour on in spite of this, and carry on the works God has inspired you to commence. But trust not to man, but depend on God alone.

Watchword ~ *Work, but be ready to quit it all the first intimation that such is God's will.*

The Deserted Pilgrims

Cecile Portaro[18] and a few of her companions made a pilgrimage to Notre-Dame-de-Drépane, in Sicily. The boat which should have brought them back started without them and they were left ashore far from Palermo, and without shelter for the night. Great was the consternation of the little band. Cecile invoked Saint Joseph and almost immediately an old man and child arrived; the former, touched by the anxiety of the holy maidens, offered to show them the way, and the child took charge of their scanty baggage. "Good man," said Cecile, "surely Saint Joseph has sent you; but we have a long way to go." "Where to?" replied the old man. "To Palermo, Rue Saint Joseph." "That is my street," rejoined the old man, and they continued their route. As soon as the little caravan had arrived at the place of their destination, the old man set down the luggage. The travellers turned round to thank him, but both old man and child had vanished, and Cecile felt sure they could be no other than Saint Joseph and the Infant Jesus.

---

18   Also known as Cecilia Portaro (died 1640), she was a Third Order Franciscan from Milan and was noted for her devotion to St. Joseph. One of her devotional practises included fasting on bread and water every Wednesday in his honour.

ॐ ☸ ॐ

21st Meditation

"But when Herod was dead, behold an Angel of the Lord appeared in sleep to Joseph in Egypt, Saying: Arise, and take the Child and His Mother, and go into the land of Israel. For they are dead that sought the life of the Child." ~ SAINT MATTHEW ii. 19, 20.

Days, weeks, months, and years pass, and the expected Angel does not reappear. What if there has been some illusion? Will it not be wise to settle definitely in Egypt? Doubtless the Jews, then so numerous in that land, often said to Joseph: Follow our example; we, like you, have given up our country and the holy city of David; like you, our hearts turn incessantly towards the Temple of our God; but nevertheless we have made our home in this friendly land.

Joseph lives from day to day, relying on the Angel's promise and awaiting his return.

Let us beware of clinging too fondly to any place, employment, or special occupation. Let us hold ourselves ready to quit all, so soon as by the voice of an angel, visible or invisible ~ I mean, by the voice of a superior, by the force of circumstance, or be secret inspiration, we shall be called to another sphere and another work.

You have conceived such and such a project, undertaken a certain work, embraced a certain state, cultivated a certain virtue, demanded a certain grace, impelled by an inspiration that you seemed divine. And now years have gone by and no light from on high has appeared, none of your hopes are realised. Your labours, your efforts, your prayers are fruitless; you begin to fear lest you have been the victim of an illusion or have taken for inspiration what was but a dream.

Ah no, it was no dream! At the moment when you least expect it, and when, like a second Tobias, you look but for death, the promised grace will be bestowed, light will come, and the star shall shine for you as it shone for the Magi, the Angel will return and announce that Herod is no more, that the obstacle which has hitherto rendered your project futile has now disappeared. All that was foreshown you is accomplished.

Watchword ~ *Cease not work, success will come in God's good time.*

22ⁿᵈ Meditation

"And Joseph arose, and took the Child and His Mother, and came into Israel." ~ SAINT MATTHEW ii. 12.

Here is another proof of Joseph's obedience. The Angel has spoken, and Joseph instantly complies with prompt and unquestioning obedience.

Each word of the narrative corresponds to some part of the Angel's message. It is with the return as with the departure; perfect conformity in the conduct of Joseph to the commands of the Angel. *Surge. Qui consurgens.* Arise. Joseph arises. ~ *Accipe puerum et matrem ejus. Accepe puerum et matrem ejus.* Take the Child and his Mother. *Vade in terram Israel. Et venit in terram Israel.* Go into the land of Israel. And he goes to the land of Israel.

This last fact is recorded in a few words, but the journey into Egypt was full of trouble and hardship. Few words suffice to record the latter fact, and yet if the Flight into Egypt was marked by pain and hardship, the Return must have been doubly so. Whether the Holy Family remained in Egypt for three, as some say, seven years, so long a journey must have been equally trying to a child who, if but three years of age, was too feeble to walk and too heavy to be carried for any length of time, and who, if as old as seven, would still be incapable of travelling fast or far.

Let us follow Joseph on this painful journey. His devotedness is inexhaustible, and his patience and serenity are equally so. Forgetful of self, he thinks only of the Mother and Child: *Accepit puerum et matrem ejus.* The way was long, and seemed interminable, but it ends at last: *Et venit in terram Israel.*

If Joseph is the protector and patron of those who are in difficulty, he is also their example, for, having experienced all kinds of embarrassment, he knows how to compassionate. Let us then have recourse to him whenever we have obstacles to encounter or difficulties that appear insurmountable.

Quod possibilitas nostra non obtinet. It is the Church herself who bids us, in such cases, have recourse to the Holy Patriarch. Following his example, let us persevere on our way, and our goal will be attained!

In face of impossibilities, do what you can and God will do the rest.

The Return to Nazareth

The Chapel of the
Little Sisters of the Poor

Two travellers from Paris, husband and wife, arrived at the Novitiate of the Little Sisters of the Poor at La Tour. They were deeply moved by the welcome they received and by the poverty that reigned in the House. The chapel struck them most forcibly; it was too small even to hold the novices, but it contained a small statue of Saint Joseph, to whom the Sisters has recourse for the funds necessary to construct a more convenient edifice. The travellers had just paid their devotions at the shrine of the Saint, when one of them said to the other: "While kneeling here an idea has struck me." ~ "And me also." ~ "We are rich." ~ "This is true." ~ "We have no children." ~ "Alas! None." ~ "What if we build on this spot a chapel in honour of Saint Joseph?" ~ "The same thought has struck me." The idea was carried out, and at the present day, thanks to the generosity of M. and Mme. Féburier, the Little Sisters of La Tour possess a beautiful church.[19]

---

19   This would be the Chapel of La Tour St. Joseph in the village of St. Pern in the north of France where the Mother House of the Little Sisters of the Poor is located. The Archbishop of Rennes blessed the first stone for these

23rd Meditation

"But hearing that Archelaus reigned in Judea in the room of Herod his father, he was afraid to go hither: and being warned in sleep, retired into the quarters of Galilee." ~ SAINT MATTHEW ii. 22.

Simplicity does not exclude prudence. He who has said, "Be harmless as the dove," has also said, "Be wise as the serpent." Faith does not dispense from the use of reason. God does not reveal everything: and if He has endowed us with intelligence, it is that we may use it. When God speaks, whether by voice of His Angels, by His Church, or by the voice of a Superior, then the part of reason is to believe and obey. On the points where the Divine Will is not revealed, then we must have recourse to the light of reason. Obedience must no longer be blind but clear sighted. Thus was it with Saint Joseph. He learns that Archelaus reigns in Herod's stead, and in his simplicity and

works of the chapel and novitiate house October 20, 1861, and consecrated in September 5, 1869. The 150th anniversary of the chapel was celebrated from October 25, 2018 to December 8, 2019.

rectitude deems that the son may be no better than the father, and fears to enter a country under the jurisdiction of this prince.

There are person who criticism, blame, and condemn everything; other who approve, excuse, and justify everything. The former lack charity, the latter are wanting in prudence; the former lack kindness of heart, and the latter are wanting in intelligence. It is true that our Lord has said, "Judge not," but Saint Paul has said, "The spiritual man judges all things." The disciple, inspired by the Holy Ghost, cannot contradict his Master.

Beware of judging rashly; beware of the spirit of criticism, for it is satanic and diabolical; but learn to discern the true from the false, good from evil, the wolf from the sheep, the true prophet from the false one, ~ if not, you will betray faith, conscience, and Jesus into the hands of the false friend, the sophist, and the politician.

After deliberate reflection, Joseph still hesitates as to what step to take, when the Angel returns, and a heavenly command terminates his suspense.

Though God only helps him who helps himself. We must trust far less to our own efforts than to Divine Assistance. The possible is for us to accomplish; God will accomplish the rest.

Watchword ~ *In face of difficulty reflect and pray.*

The Holy Family and the Society of Jesus

Three novices of the Society of Jesus[20] whilst making a pilgrimage, lost their way, and though exhausted by hunger and fatigue, ceased not to pray and trust to heaven for help. Their hope was realised. They saw a man and a woman approach, the latter bearing in her arms a child. "Come with us," said the stranger; "you have lost your way, we shall direct you, but first you must take some refreshment, for you seem exhausted." Saying this they shared their own provisions with the novices.

The repast was delicious, and heightened by the affability of the hosts. The novices, though overwhelmed by astonishment and gratitude, were anxious to know to whom they were indebted for such kind hospitality. Their curiosity was gratified when one of the three strangers said: "We are the founders of the Society of Jesus: *Nos fundavimus Societatem Jesu.*" They then vanished, and the novices then knew that they were the Holy Family.

---

20 The Jesuits.

Holy Family with a Bird

24th Meditation

"And coming, He dwelt in a city called Nazareth: that it might be fulfilled which was said by the prophets, that He should be called a Nazarite." ~ *SAINT MATTEW ii. 23.*

Even here on earth we may hope for happiness. But it must be purchased by long and painful trials, and tempered by the expectation of others, not less bitter and not less certain to arrive. Nevertheless, whatever happens, if, like Saint Joseph, you have Jesus and Mary with you, you will be happy. Picture to yourself Saint Joseph in Nazareth. His life is calm, simple, and uniform; laborious, it is true, hard, rough, and never free from solicitude, for tomorrow's bread depends on the labour of today. Still sufficient to the day is the evil thereof, and work is sweet when it is for Jesus, and with Jesus that it is done.

Who shall recount the charm of that home in Nazareth? Listen to the questions the Divine Child addresses to His Mother and to His adopted father. Note the wise and modest replies of Mary and of St. Joseph, and their sweet satisfaction at the sight of the respectful approval with which their words are greeted by the Holy Child.

In these discourses little is said, much is heard; they listen intently to that inner voice which echoes to the outer word.

Let us seek even here below that calm, peace, and tranquillity which are a foretaste of heaven, and make a paradise of earth. In thought and heart let us live with Jesus, Mary and Joseph, and there, even amid trials, labour, and care, we shall enjoy that peace which the world cannot give, which the world does not know, that peace which no storm can disturb, and which emanates from the presence of Jesus, of Mary and of Joseph.

Watchword ~ _Let your life and conversation be with the Holy Family._

Confession Made Good, Thanks to Saint Joseph

A young woman, having unhappily broken her vow of chastity, had not the courage to confess it; and with the profanation of the sacraments, her life became one of torment and remorse. She at last resolved to have recourse to Saint Joseph, and during nine days devoutly recited the hymn and prayer to the Saint. The novena ended, her false shame vanished, and, as she expressed herself in a letter to Perè de Barry: "Far from being painful, her confession was a real happiness."[21] She adds: "Convinced by this experience of the power and goodness of Saint Joseph, I resolved to wear his medal night and day, and from that moment I have been enabled to resist every impure temptation, and have received favours so innumerable that I know not how adequately to express my gratitude."

❧❀❦

---

21   Fr. de Barry was a Jesuit from the 17th who was responsible for reviving devotion to St. Joseph in Avignon. Through him a chapel for St. Joseph was established in each of the parishes and a children's Mass was instituted on March 19. In the college he had formed a congregation of St. Joseph and every Wednesday evening held a service in his honour. The Jesuit Fathers of Avignon were particularly attached to this saint as a result.

25th Meditation

"And His parents went every year to Jerusalem, at the solemn day of the pasch." ~ SAINT LUKE ii. 41.

The Holy Ghost delights in recalling the adoptive paternity of Joseph: *Et ibant Parentes ejus*, his parents. The holy Patriarch is placed in the same rank as the Blessed Virgin, and this because Saint Joseph's feelings towards Jesus were the feelings of a father, and those of Jesus for Joseph were the affections of a son.

How admirable the simplicity of the Holy Family! Externally there is nothing remarkable to be discerned ~ Jesus, Mary, and Joseph fulfil but the ordinary duties of their calling. They do simply what all the faithful observers of the law do; nothing more and nothing less. In nothing are they to be distinguished from an ordinary person. They neither fall short of nor exceed in the performance of their duty.

How different is our conduct to theirs! We dream of ideal perfection, multiply our devotions, but neglect the essential practise of religion and the elementary duties of Christian life. We aspire to evangelical counsels and neglect the commandments! Let us beware of any inspiration that urges us to the accomplishment of anything extraordinary whilst we fail in the courage necessary for the fulfilment of the ordinary duties of life.

First let us faithfully comply with the requirements of the common law: *Ibant per singulos annos.* If God has destined us for some wonderful mission He will manifest it in His own good time. Neither let us seek occasions of sacrifice; God will demand that at the fitting time, and make it conduce to His glory and to our own.

__Watchword__ ~ *Fulfil first the ordinary duties of life.*

__*Conversion Due to Saint Joseph*__

A Christian woman had a daughter whose conduct was truly deplorable. The poor mother never entered the church without prostrating herself before a picture of Saint Joseph, and demanding with tears the conversion of her child. At last the idea entered her mind to present her daughter with a picture of Saint Joseph. She at once seized the opportunity of her daughter's absence and went instantly to her room. On the table was a book. But what a book! "Ah! Saint Joseph," said the mother, "forgive me if I place your picture here, but necessity compels me." The young girl on her return home took up the book to read. "Why, what is this?" she exclaimed, "a picture!" She looked again, then turned it over and began to read mechanically a prayer printed in verse. Then she burst into tears; threw her bad book into the fire. She was converted.

ॐ ❀ ॐ

26th Meditation

"And when He was twelve years old, they going up to Jerusalem, according to the custom of the Feast, and having fulfilled the days, when they returned, the child Jesus remained in Jerusalem; and His parents knew it not." ~ SAINT LUKE 11. 42, 43.

And his parents knew it not! Of what were Mary and Joseph thinking? ~ Of Jesus. Most likely that, in accordance with the usual custom, Joseph was in company of the men and Mary in that of the women. The age of Jesus would admit His travelling with either party. Joseph thought that the Child was with Mary, and Mary imagined Him with Joseph.

Why, then, did the Divine Child take advantage of this circumstance, and cause His parents such poignant grief? First, He wished to afford them an opportunity of evincing the depth of their love. He Himself will give the second reason.

Often, without fault of ours, Jesus hides Himself from our sight. He leaves us alone; we remain indifferent to prayer, and void of energy in His service. A vague and indefinable disquietude possesses us. Let us not be cast down. The greatest saints have all, even as Joseph and Mary, passed through the same trial.

Watchword ~ *In the hour of trial, fear not.*

Conversion due to Saint Joseph

A young man who had been taken to Paris to perfect himself in his trade, returned home, having lost both faith and health. His mother and his sister pray earnestly for his conversion. The month of St. Joseph arrives, and an oratory is prepared in honour of the Saint. The young free-thinker asked his sister the reason of these preparations. She replies, "It is the month of Saint Joseph, and we are going to pray for your conversion." The youth began to laugh, but remained listening to the reading which formed part of the devotions, then, uncovering his head, he exclaimed, "Ah, my poor sister, how miserable I am! What a wretch I have become, for I no longer know how to pray! Teach me, for I wish to live as a Christian." The wish was soon complied with, and the genuineness of the young man's conversion was evident in the patience with which he endured the acute suffering of a fatal disease, which he accepted in expiation of his faults, and which after a few months conducted him to heaven.

27ᵗʰ Meditation

"And thinking that He was in the company, they came a day's journey, and sought Him among their kinsfolk and acquaintance." ~ *SAINT LUKE ii. 44.*

Joseph and Mary seek for Jesus at first among their friends and acquaintance. This was a natural thing to do, and they were right in hoping to find Him there.

Are you afflicted? Seek consolation among your friends and acquaintance. Nothing is more natural, nothing more reasonable; and therefore, save in case of a special interposition of Providence, nothing is more in conformity with the divine will. In acting thus you will frequently meet with the consolation of which you stand in need, but not always so, for at time your hopes will be frustrated. God wills us to act in accordance with the rules of human prudence, and to employ all natural means; then, when we have fulfilled our part, inspiration and light will come to direct us in the right way, and enable us to accomplish our desires.

<u>Watchword</u> ~ *Help yourself, and God will help you.*

<u>Saint Joseph and the Gift of Prayer</u>

Père de Barry mentions an instance of a young woman who, finding great difficulty in prayer, made a novena to Saint Joseph, and from that time found great consolation in the sacred exercise.

The same father adds: "I have met with so souls so closely united to God that, whatever their occupation, they never lose sight of the Divine Presence. I have asked, Whence came this grace? And one and all have given me the same reply ~ "We owe it to Saint Joseph."

❧ ✿ ☙

28th Meditation

"And not finding Him, they returned into Jerusalem, seeking Him. And it came to pass, that after three days they found Him in the temple, sitting in the midst of the doctors, bearing them and asking them questions." ~ SAINT LUKE ii. 45, 46.

Return to Jerusalem, enter the temple, have recourse to prayer, and you will find Jesus. But you must also seek and act. Joseph and Mary return to Jerusalem, but even on their way they do not relax in their search for the Divine Child.

At last they find Him. Ah! With what astonishment is Joseph overwhelmed. He has, by keeping silence, veiled the divinity of Jesus, and now, behold the Divine Child betrays Himself by the surprising wisdom of His questions and His replies.

Such circumstances as these are rare, and must serve as preceding only in obedience to inspiration or a special command, and then only if the glory of God requires it. Our habitual inclination should be to the quiet and retirement of a hidden life.

As soon as Joseph and Mary appear,

Jesus quits His astonished audience and rejoins His mother and His adopted father.

What tongue can tell their joy at hearing again the sweet dear voice of the Divine Child, and beholding His loving gaze! Who shall tell their consolation when they behold Him quit all to join them, thus showing that they were dearer to Him than all aught else on earth!

Let us be persistent in our search, unwearied in our entreaties, then shall we, in answer to our prayer, find Jesus in Jerusalem, in the temple, in the midst of the doctors. He withdraws but for a time, in order to teach and prove us.

Watchword ~ *To action and Prayer*

Saint Joseph and Prayer

A poor religious was unable to meditate without being assailed by the most violent distractions. She had recourse to Saint Joseph, and her troubles ceased. Whenever she contemplated the perfections of the holy patriarch, she was lost in admiration, her slightest wish was granted; for instance, did she desire to rise earlier than usual, she had only to ask Saint Joseph's help, and she would awake at the desired time.

29th Meditation

"And all that heard Him were astonished at His wisdom and His answers.   And seeing Him they wondered.   And His Mother said to Him: Son, why hast Thou done so to us?   Behold, Thy father and I have sought Thee sorrowing." ~ SAINT LUKE ii. 47, 48

Joseph is here recognised by Mary as being the adopted father of Jesus, and by His silence Jesus acknowledges him as father, who exercises all the authority and undertakes all the cares of the parental office. Joseph shares all Mary's grief, wonder, and joy. The hour of trial is over, and consolation has arrived, a consolation mingled with wondering admiration at the way in which God has made trial and affliction redound to His glory and that of His tried ones. The joy is tempered by some admixture of austerity. It would almost seem as if Jesus reproached Mary and Joseph for their tender solicitude and anxiety at His absence. Impossible that such could be the case. It is not a reproach, but a respectful and gentle explanation, that Jesus gives. It is a child justifying himself for conduct that at first sight appears so strange. Jesus seems to say: "Is it possible I could have left you had not the glory of my Heavenly Father demanded it? No obligation less powerful, less sacred, could ever have withdrawn me from your loving presence: *Neciebatis, Did you not know it?*"

When the glory of God requires it, forsake all sacrifice, even your warmest and most lawful affections.

<u>Watchword</u> ~ *Seek first the glory of God.*

<u>Success in Missions</u>

Père Antoine Natal,[22] of the Society of

---

22   Possibly a reference to Fr. Antonio Natale (1648-1701). Born in Palermo on April 3, 1648. After formed in the flourishing Marian Congregation 'del Fervore' and finishing two years of philosophy, he entered the Society of Jesus on June 17, 1663. Once he completed his literary and philosophical studies, he was sent to various small colleges in Sicily to teach grammar and rhetoric, offices in which he was tried greatly and as a result set a remarkable example of character. He became a priest and was sent to Salemi, Alcamo and Palermo where he took care of young Jesuit students. In 1690 he finally became rector of the novitiate in Messina and master of novices. Two years later he obtained permission to be relieved of these duties and was sent to Palermo to

Jesus, had a great devotion to Saint Joseph, and published a book in honour of the Saint. Unwearied in his missionary labours, he ensured their success by placing them under the patronage of Saint Joseph, and offered him daily homage by the recitation of a chapter of prayer he had composed in honour of the Saint.

---

direct the Marian Congregation, a duty with which he took considerable care and that bore much fruit. He was not only the spiritual father of the house but also the confessor of the archbishop of Palermo, Ferdinando Bazan (born c. 1626-1702), and as such extended his influence to the entire island, especially through the younger generations. He was also entrusted with the direction of the Interior Missions of a part of Sicily. He showed rare examples of virtue and became renowned for holiness. He died in Palermo after suffering a painful illness October 17, 1701. He also wrote several works, two of his most noteworthy are: 1) "Glorie del Sacerdotio rivelate a S. Brigida insieme coi suoi obblighi e pregiuditii" ('Glories of the Priesthood Revealed to St. Bridget together with its duties and obligations'), Palermo, 1693- 2) "Il Paradiso in terra, spalancato a chi vuole ed è libero a scegliere il più securo stato di vita", ('Paradise on earth opened to all; or, A religious vocation the surest way in life'), Palermo, 1699. This particular work proved very popular and enjoyed several translations. Unfortunately, his book on St. Joseph does not seem to be remembered in our times, except for what Fr. Boylesve has told us above. No doubt the example Fr. Boylesve wished to show in mentioning Fr. Antoine is how successful his work became due to his great devotion to St. Joseph.

30th Meditation

"Is not this the carpenter's Son?"
~ SAINT MATTHEW xiii. 55.

"Is not this the carpenter?" ~
SAINT MARK vi. 3.

"Is not this Jesus, the son of
Joseph, whose father and mother we
know?" ~ SAINT JOHN vi. 42

These appellations meet with no objection on the part of Jesus. Enough has been said by Him to show that God is His real Father; but Joseph, being His Heavenly Father's representative, Spouse of Mary and head of the Family, Jesus acknowledges him as His adopted father. He heeds not being called the carpenter's son; there is nothing in that to humiliate or give offence. Joseph is no man for whom to blush.

These words, the last mention of Saint Joseph in the Gospel, show forth his most glorious title, his greatness, and his virtue. His greatness, for he fills the office of father to

Jesus; his virtue, for he is worthy of this dignity, and Jesus is content to pass as Joseph's son.

Remain in the sphere in which Providence has placed you. Follow the example of Joseph. The glory of Jesus shines forth the brighter for Joseph's humility. Had our Lord's adopted father been a man of learning and position, we should have marvelled less at the wondrous words that proceed from his lips.

God's share in our actions is but rendered the more conspicuous by the lowliness of our position and the mediocrity of our talents. But, as with Joseph, so with us; and though we are but the instrument, and to God is due all the glory, some portion of it will be reflected on us.

Watchword ~ *Fulfil the duties of your state, and by so doing you will glorify God.*

Saint Joseph and the Papal Zouave

Joseph la Saige de la Villebrune, lieutenant in the Papal army,[23] had a tender devotion to Saint Joseph, and was not forgotten by the Saint. As his last hour drew nigh, he sent for the chaplain, saying: Saint Joseph bids me confess at once, as I have not a moment to lose. After hearing his confession, the chaplain announced that he was going to

---

23   The Papal Zouaves were an infantry force formed in defence of the Papal States. They first started as a unit in 1860 under Louis Juchault de Lamoricière in 1860 and were called the France-Belgian Tirailleurs. Tirailleurs were light infantry sent to skirmish ahead of the main column. In January of 1861 they changed their name to the Papal Zouaves. The Zouaves mostly consisted of unmarried Catholic men who volunteered to assist Bl. Pius IX against the Italian unificationist Risorgimento.

Lieutenant Joseph la Saige de la Villebrune was born in Rennes on August 25, 1837. He entered Saint-François-Xavier college in 1850 and enlisted on May 29, 1860. He became a Corporal on June 17, 1860, then a Sergeant on August 27 that same year, finally becoming Lieutenant in 1861. He was awarded the Cross of Pius IX on October 18, 1860 and also the Medal pro Pétri sede, December 25, 1860. Fought at Castelfldardo and in the battle of Passo di Correze, January 25, 1861. He died of illness in Marine, February 25, 1862. A monograph of his final moments and his devotion to St. Joseph can be found in the Bibliothèque Nationale de France. (BnF, département Philosophie, histoire, sciences de l'homme, 8-LN27-11815). He is not to be confused with the politician of the same name (1774-1833) who lived and died earlier than the formation of the Zouaves.

say Mass for the sick man, and would afterwards bring him the Holy Communion. Just as the chaplain was about to ascend the steps of the altar, Saint Joseph sent to say that there was no time to be lost; he recited aloud the prayers for Communion, thanking God for permitting him to retain his consciousness so long.

When he had finished praying his delirium returned, but even then he opened his eyes only to turn them towards the image of the Saint; he even wished to throw himself on his knees before his holy patron, saying to the sisters, when they tried to persuade him to lie down again: "Give me my clothes quickly; do you not see that Saint Joseph is waiting for me?"

On the morrow, about three o'clock in the morning, he opened his eyes, fixed them on his patron, and gently passed away.

ॐ ❁ ॐ

31st Meditation

"And was subject unto them." ~
SAINT LUKE ii. 51

Jesus yields obedience to Saint Joseph and the order of things seem reversed. Henceforth, what pretext will you find to dispense you from obeying? But I am wiser and better than is he who is placed over me as my superior. That may be, or it may not be so. The wisdom and sanctity of Jesus are incomparable, and yet Joseph commands and Jesus obeys.

Joseph commands Jesus! Kings have but men for their subjects. Joseph is more than king; true that but one subject forms his empire, but this subject is King of kings, and King of Angels, the God made man: *Et erat subditus illis.*

Joseph is surpassed by none! Placed between God and man, interpreter and instrument of the Divinity. Joseph, as prophet, transmits the divine message to people and kings. As being, in a certain sense, intermediary between God the Father and God the Son, Joseph is interpreter and instrument of the Eternal Father, and transmits the divine

commands not to kings or nation but to Him who is the Monarch of all!

Can the sacerdotal dignity equal that of Joseph? From the throne of truth itself, Peter, living and infallible in the person of his successors, pronounces on faith, on morals. Prophet and king, the Holy Father teaches and commands; no earthly dignity so great as his, no function so sublime, save that of Joseph. Joseph speaks; and He who is power and wisdom, Jesus, the God Incarnate, obeys.

In heaven the saints do not lose the privileges granted to them on earth. Whilst here below, Joseph commanded Jesus; in heaven he turns his suppliant gaze on Jesus, and at once his prayers are answered. On earth Jesus obeyed Joseph, in heaven He forestalls His adopted father's slightest wish.

Have recourse, then, to Joseph. ~ *Ite ad Joseph.* He is all-powerful with Jesus.

Watchword ~ *Do God's will, and God will strengthen yours.*

St. Joseph's Power with our Lord

Catherine de Saint-Augustin,[24] hospital sister in Quebec, beheld in vision, on the Feast of the Ascension, Our Lord's entry into heaven. St. Joseph took precedence of the saints of the Old Testament. It was he who presented the King of Glory to His Eternal Father. Our Lord at the same time declared that in heaven He would continue to do the will of His adopted father.

∂⊛⌐

24　Bl. Mary Catherine of St. Augustine, OSA, (1632-1668) (French: *Marie-Catherine de Saint-Augustin*) was a French canoness regular who was instrumental in the development of the Hôtel-Dieu de Québec in service to the colony of New France. She was a victim soul, was physically beaten by the devils, and also had many visions of Our Lord, Our Lady, St. Joseph, St. Michael, also souls from Purgatory. She was beatified in 1989.

Saint Joseph and the Sacred Heart

Picture to yourself Saint Joseph bearing in one hand a lily ~ symbol of chastity ~ and with the other pointing out the Infant Jesus, who is standing on the knees of His adopted father. The Divine Child points to St. Joseph, and from His smiling lips seem to issue these words written beneath the picture:

"He has carried Me in his arms, pressed Me to his heart, maintained Me by his labour ~ what can I refuse him?"

If a momentary repose on the Heart of Our Lord transformed Saint John into the Apostle of Love, what must it have been with him who, in loving embrace, so often held the Divine Child pressed closely to his heart?

᪔ ❀ ᪔

Pius IX and Saint Joseph

Above the *prie-Dieu*[25] of the Holy Father was a beautiful picture representing Saint Joseph with with the Infant Jesus in his arms. The Divine Child reveals His heart, and seems to pronounce the words inscribed beneath the picture: *Ite ad Joseph* ~ Go to Joseph.

It was here, at the feet of Saint Joseph, that the Vicar of Christ commended the Universal Church to the care of the Divine child.

కు⁂సం

Decree of Pius IX

In the same way that God established Joseph, the son of the Patriarch Jacob, Governor of all the land of Egypt, in order to insure to the people the necessary means of subsistence, so when the times were fulfilled for the Eternal Father to send His only Son to redeem the world, He chose another Joseph, of whom the first was the type; He made him

---

25 I.e. a prayer kneeler.

lord and master of His house and His goods, and elected him as guardian of His principal treasures. And Joseph was espoused to the Immaculate Virgin Mary from whom, by the power of the Holy Ghost, was born our Lord Jesus Christ, who deigned to be reputed the Son of Joseph, and was subject unto him. And He, whom so many kings and prophets desired to see, Joseph no only beheld, but conversed with Him, held Him in his arms with paternal affection, embraced Him, watched with care over His maintenance, and provided for the nurture of Him, who was to be the spiritual nourishment of His faithful people, and the bread of eternal life.

In consequence of this sublime dignity conferred by God on His most faithful servant, the Church has always held Saint Joseph in the highest honour, after the Most Holy Virgin, his spouse; has continually sung his praises, and has had recourse to him, by preference, in her greatest distress. And as in these sad days the Church is assailed on all side by her enemies, and oppressed by such misfortunes that the impious are persuaded that the time is come when the gates of hell shall prevail against her, the venerable bishops of the entire Catholic world have humbly prayed the Sovereign Pontiff, in their name and in that of all the faithful confided to their care, to deign to declare Saint Joseph patron of the Catholic Church. This petition having been renewed with still greater urgency at the time of the Ecumenical Vatican Council, our Holy Father Pius IX, profoundly moved at the late deplorable events, and wishing to place himself and all the faithful in a special manner under the all-powerful patronage of the holy Patriarch Saint Joseph, has deigned to grant the petition of the venerable Bishops. For this reason he has solemnly declared Saint Joseph Patron of the Catholic Church; he has decreed that the Feast of this Saint, on the 19th of March, should be henceforth raised to the position of a double of the first class, though without octave, on account of Lent. He has also prescribed that the declaration thus made by the present decree of the Sacred Congregation of Rites should be published on the day consecrated to the Immaculate Conception of the Virgin Mother of God, the spouse of the most chaste Saint Joseph; whatever to the contrary notwithstanding.

The 8th December of the year 1870.

St. Theresa and St. Joseph

"I have chosen as advocate and intercessor the glorious Saint Joseph, and recommend myself constantly to his protection. ... I never remember having asked from him any favour that he has not granted."

❧ ✿ ❧

Novena to St. Joseph

Recite daily one of the prayers, and meditate on one of the following subjects:

1st Day ~ As Saint John Baptist, so too was Saint Joseph sanctified from his mother's womb. ~ *Gerson*

2nd Day ~ I regard as pious and correct the opinion of those who consider that in merit and greatness Saint Joseph far excels all other saints. ~ *Suarez*

3rd Day ~ God has reunited in St. Joseph all the light and splendour of the other saints. ~ *Saint Gregory de Nanzianzum*

4th Day ~ Of all men, Saint Joseph was the only one selected to co-operate in carrying out the grandest work of the Divinity.

5th Day ~ Even as Our Lady was "blessed among women," so Saint Joseph was blessed among men. ~ *Navæus*

6th Day ~ He was greater than Patriarchs or Prophets, for he was the spouse of Our Lady and foster father of our Lord Jesus Christ. ~ *Tolet*

7th Day ~ He was head of God's family on earth, the first disciple of our Lord, most exact imitator of His virtues, first in the confidence of Jesus and of Mary, and under the new covenant, the first to suffer persecution for righteousness' sake. ~ *Rupert*

8th Day ~ His purity equalled that of the highest angels. ~ *Saint Francis de Sales*

9th Day ~ Only after death, the other Saints enjoy the felicity of Heaven; Joseph, happier than they, possesses God even on earth, and the Divine Child is dependent on his loving care. ~ *Rupert*

Close of Novena ~ When a husband or a father entreats, such entreaty is a command to a wife or child; therefore take Saint Joseph as your patron, friend, and most powerful intercessor. ~ *Gerson*

❧ ❀ ❧

Prayers to Saint Joseph

Let us address Saint Joseph in the words of the Angel: ~ "Joseph, son of David, fear not to take unto thee Mary thy wife, for that which is conceived in her is of the Holy Ghost." ~ SAINT MATTHEW i. 20.

Let us address Saint Joseph in the words of the Church: ~ "We beseech Thee, O Lord, that we may be assisted by the merits of the spouse of Thy most holy Mother, that what of ourselves we are unable to obtain, may be given us by his intercession."

❦ ✾ ❧

FOR PRIESTS

Prayers to Saint Joseph

Ante Missam: O felicem virum, beatum Joseph, cui datum est Deum, quem multi reges voluerunt videre et non viderunt, audire et non audierunt, non solum videre et audire, sed portare, deosculari, vestire et custodire.

V. Ora pro nobis, beate Joseph.
R. Ut digni efficamur promissionibus Christi.

(O happy are you, O blessed Joseph, to whom God has given He Whom many kings longed to see and saw not; to hear and heard not; but also to carry Him, to embrace Him, to clothe Him, and to guard Him. **V.** Pray for us, Blessed Joseph **R**: That we may be made worthy of the promises of Christ.)[*]

(An indulgence of one year to priests who recite this prayer before Mass.)

---

[*]   This English translation was not in the original book. The translations for the following prayers were.

ಎಲ್ಘಿ

Post Missam et per Diem

Virginum custos et pater, sancte Joseph, cuus fideli custodiæ ipsa innocentia Christus Jesus, et Virgo virginum Maria commissa fuit: te per hoc utrumque charissimum pignus, Jesus et Mariam, obsecro et obtestor, ut me ab omni immunditia præservatum, mente incontaminata, puro corde, et casto corpore, Jesu et Mariæ semper facias castissime famulari. Amen.

(An indulgence of one year to priests each time they recite this prayer.
Also an **Efficacious Prayer for the Faithful**)

(Translation:) Holy Joseph, father and protector of virgins, faithful guardian to whom God confided Jesus, Innocence itself, and Mary, the Virgin of virgins, by this twofold treasure I implore Thee to preserve me pure in body and in soul, so that I may serve Jesus and Mary in perfect chastity. Amen.

ಎಲ್ಘಿ

Memorare to Saint Joseph

Remember, O most holy Joseph, that never was it known that any one who fled to thy protection, implored thy help and sought thy intercession, was left unaided. Inspired with this confidence, I come to thee, O Foster-Father of the Word Incarnate. Despise not my petition, but in thy mercy hear and answer me. Amen.

Indulgence of 300 days. ~ Pius IX. 1869.

❧ ✤ ❧

Litany to Saint Joseph

Lord, Have mercy on us.
Christ, have mercy on us.
Lord, have mercy on us.
Christ, hear us.
Christ, graciously hear us.
God the Father of Heaven,
  Have mercy on us.
God the Son, Redeemer of the world,
  Have mercy on us.
God the Holy Ghost,
  Have mercy on us.

Holy Trinity, one God,
  Have mercy on us.

*Holy Mary, Spouse of Saint Joseph,
                    pray for us, (etc.)*
*Holy Joseph, son of David,
*Saint Joseph, chaste Spouse of the Virgin
        Mary,
*Saint Joseph, Guardian of the Holy
        Family,
*Saint Joseph, nursing Father of Jesus,
*Saint Joseph, Protector of Jesus and Mary,
*Saint Joseph, humble artisan,
*Saint Joseph, good and faithful servant,
*Saint Joseph, whom God declared just,
*Saint Joseph, humble imitation
   of Jesus and Mary,
*Saint Joseph, proved by God,
*Saint Joseph, ever submissive
   to the Divine Will,
*Saint Joseph, model of humility,
*Saint Joseph, Spotless Lily,
*Saint Joseph, Patron of the
   Interior or hidden life,
*Saint Joseph, Help of the Church,
*Saint Joseph, dispenser of grace,
*Saint Joseph, our Protector,
*Saint Joseph, who didst die in the arms
   of Jesus and Mary,
*Saint Joseph, aid of the dying,

*Saint Joseph, patron of a happy death,

Lamb of God, who takest away
the sins of the world.
  Spare us, O Lord!
Lamb of God, who takest away
 the sins of the world,
  Graciously hear us O Lord!
Lamb of God, who takest away
 the sins of the world,
  Have mercy on us!
Christ hear us.
Christ graciously hear us.

    V. Pray for us, Saint Joseph.
      R. That we may be made worthy of the
      promises of Christ.

Let us pray. Grant, we beseech Thee, O Lord, that we may be assisted by the merits of the spouse of thy most Holy Virgin Mother, that what of ourselves we cannot obtain, may be granted us through His intercession. Who livest and reignest with the Father and the Holy Ghost, world without end. Amen.

❧ ✤ ❧

THE THREE INVOCATIONS

Jesus, Mary, Joseph, I give you my heart, my soul and my life.

Jesus, Mary, Joseph, assist me in my last agony.

Jesus, Mary, Joseph, may I die in peace in your most holy company.

❧ ✤ ❧

APPENDIX

Additional Devotions to St. Joseph not included in the original book by Fr. de Boylesve.

The 'Four Visits' Novena

In the 4th Meditation, Fr. de Boylesve mentioned the story of Fr. Lallemand and the two professors to whom he promised would receive a particular grace from St. Joseph if they spread devotion to him among their students. One of the professors then wanted to exchange his request for another grace, but St. Joseph so speedily granted his original petition for the grace to write worthily of Our Lord it was too late to exchange the request!

However, Fr. de Boylesve did not mention Fr. Lallemand had the two professors also say a Nine Day Novena to St. Joseph of his own invention, the 'Four Visits' Novena.

Originally, Fr. Lallemand devised a simple way to make four interior spiritual 'visits' to honour St. Joseph: for nine days one must simply 'visit' four particular attributes of St. Joseph throughout the day for each of the nine days. During each visit, consider the various attributes of St. Joseph's love and fidelity, remembering to thank God for honouring St. Joseph and, through his intercession, request a similar grace:

1st Visit ~ St. Joseph's Fidelity to Grace; the Holy Ghost's action in his soul.

2nd Visit ~ St. Joseph's Fidelity to the Interior Life; his Spirit of Recollection.

3rd Visit~ St. Joseph's Love for Our Lady.

4th Visit ~ St. Joseph's Love for the Divine Child.

How to Make this Novena

These interior 'visits' may be made anywhere – at home, at work, on the street, in the car or bus – and at any time. There is no time restriction, they do not 'have' to be made at a particular time each day, as long as the four visits are made through the day for nine consecutive days. For example, you can split the four meditations for morning, noon, afternoon and evening, or, do two in the morning, two in the afternoon, etc., whenever is convenient to fulfil the four visits. This Novena is most efficacious when combined with efforts to spread devotion to St. Joseph and make him loved.

During the first visit, consider St. Joseph's fidelity to grace. Meditate upon the action of the Holy Ghost in his soul. At the conclusion of this brief meditation, thank God for honouring St. Joseph, and ask through his intercession for a similar grace.

Later in the day, consider St. Joseph's fidelity to the interior life. Study his spirit of interior recollection. Meditate upon this, thank God for the honour given to St. Joseph, and ask for a similar grace.

Later still in the day, consider St. Joseph's love for Our Lady. Meditate on this, thank God, and ask for a similar grace.

Finally, in a fourth visit, reflect upon St. Joseph's love for the Divine Child. Meditate on this, thank God, and ask for a similar grace.

~ **Prayers for the Conclusion of Each Visit (optional)** ~

While Fr. Lallemand apparently did not compose specific meditations or prayers for each 'visit', you may conclude each visit with a prayer to St. Joseph of your choosing, or perhaps the following prayer:

"O great and good St. Joseph, chaste spouse of Immaculate Mary, and guardian of the Word Incarnate, we place ourselves with confidence under thy protection, and beg of thee to teach us to practise the virtues of the Child Jesus. We thank God for the singular favours He was pleased to bestow upon thee, and we earnestly desire to become pure, and humble, and patient, like unto thee. Pray, then for us, St. Joseph, and through that love which thou hast for Jesus and Mary, and which they have for thee, obtain for us the invaluable blessing of living and dying in the love of Jesus, Mary, and thee. Amen."

❧ ✿ ☙

Devotion of the Seven Joys
and the Seven Sorrows of St. Joseph

As seen in the pious reflection recounted in the 19th Mediation, two Franciscan friars were shipwrecked off the coast of Flanders and clung to a plank for dear life. After several days at sea they at last thought to pray to St. Joseph for help. A beautiful youth appeared and steered them to shore. The friars threw themselves at the feet of the youth and begged him to reveal his name. "I am Joseph, whom you invoked, and if you wish to give me pleasure, let no day pass without reciting seven Paters and Aves (I.e. Our Fathers and Hail Marys) in memory of the seven joys and seven dolours of my earthly life." He then disappeared.

The following is a devotion of the Seven Joys and Sorrows composed by Bl. Januarius Sarnelli, C.S.S.R. (1702-1744), friend of St. Alphonsus de Liguori and one his earliest companions in the founding years of the Redemptorists. The Glory Be has been included to the Our Fathers and Hail Marys to be said.

1: **First Sorrow: The trial of St. Joseph.**

"But Joseph her husband, being a just man, and not wishing to expose her to reproach, was minded to put her away privately." (Matt. 1:19)

First Joy: The message of the Angel.

"But while he thought on these things, behold, an angel of the Lord appeared to him in a dream, saying, "Do not be afraid, Joseph, son of David, to take to you Mary your wife, for that which is begotten in her is of the Holy Spirit." (Matt. 1:20)

O chaste Spouse of Mary most holy, glorious St. Joseph, great was the trouble and anguish of your heart when you wert minded to put away privately your inviolate Spouse, yet your joy was unspeakable when the surpassing mystery of the Incarnation was made known to you by the Angel! By this sorrow and this joy, we beseech you to comfort our souls, both now and in the sorrows of our final hour, with the joy of a good life and a holy death after the pattern of your own, in the arms of Jesus and Mary.

Our Father . . . Hail Mary . . . Glory be . . .

2. Second Sorrow: The poverty of Jesus' birth. "And she brought forth her first born son, and wrapped him in swaddling clothes, and laid him in a manger, because there was no room for them in the inn." (Luke 2:7)

Second Joy: The birth of the Saviour. "And the angel said to them, "Do not be afraid, for behold, I bring you good news of great joy which shall be to all people; for today in the town of David, a Saviour has been born to you, who is Christ the Lord." (Luke 2:10-11)

O most blessed Patriarch, glorious St. Joseph, who was chosen to be the foster father of the Word made flesh, your sorrow at seeing the Child Jesus born in such poverty was suddenly changed into heavenly exultation when you did hear the angelic hymn and beheld the glories of that resplendent night. By this sorrow and this joy, we implore you to obtain for us the grace to pass over from life's pathway to hear the angelic songs of praise, and to rejoice in the shining splendour of celestial glory.

Our Father . . . Hail Mary . . . Glory be . . .

3. Third Sorrow: The Circumcision.

"And when eight days were fulfilled for his circumcision, his name was called Jesus, the name given to him by the angel before he was conceived in the womb." (Luke 2:21)

Third Joy: The Holy Name of Jesus.

"And he did not know her until she brought forth her first born son. And he called his name Jesus." (Matt. 1:25)

O glorious St. Joseph you faithfully obeyed the law of God, and your heart was pierced at the sight of the Precious Blood that was shed by the Infant Saviour during His Circumcision, but the Name of Jesus gave you new life and filled you with quiet joy. By this sorrow and this joy, obtain for us the grace to be freed from all sin during life, and to die rejoicing, with the holy Name of Jesus in our hearts and on our lips.

Our Father . . . Hail Mary . . . Glory be . . .

4. Fourth Sorrow: The prophecy of Simeon.

"And Simeon blessed them, and said to Mary his mother, "Behold this child is destined for the fall and the rise of many in Israel, and for a sign that shall be contradicted. And your own soul a sword shall pierce." (Luke 2:34)

Fourth Joy: The effects of the Redemption.

"And coming up at that very hour, she began to give praise to the Lord, and spoke of him to all who were awaiting the redemption of Jerusalem." (Luke 2:38)

O most faithful Saint who shared the mysteries of our Redemption, glorious St. Joseph, the prophecy of Simeon regarding the sufferings of Jesus and Mary caused you to shudder with mortal dread, but at the same time filled you with a blessed joy for the salvation and glorious resurrection which he foretold, would be attained by countless souls. By this sorrow and this joy, obtain for us that we may be among the number of those who, through the merits of Jesus and the intercession of Mary the Virgin Mother, are predestined to a glorious resurrection.

Our Father . . . Hail Mary . . . Glory be . . .

5. Fifth Sorrow: The flight into Egypt.
"So he arose, and took the child and his mother by night, and withdrew into Egypt." (Matt. 2:14)

Fifth Joy: The overthrow of the idols of Egypt. "The burden of Egypt. Behold the Lord will ascend upon a swift cloud and will enter into Egypt, and the idols of Egypt will be moved at his presence, and the heart of Egypt shall melt in the midst thereof." (Is. 19:1)**

** *Overthrow of the Idols:* Theologians believe that the Holy Family took the road through Gaza into Egypt and went in the direction of Heliopolis, which tradition states was their place of residence there. Ven. Mary of Agreda says that the flight into Egypt was not only to escape from Herod, but to also to fulfil the prophecies of the Old Testament, such as that stated in the passage of Isaiah above in that the idols would be moved in Egypt. Ven. Mary of Agreda says before the Holy Family settled in Heliopolis they were led by angelic guidance through various places so the Lord could pour His blessings on the land and cast out the demons occupying the temples of the idols and receiving sacrifices from the inhabitants who thought they were praying to gods. Every village was filled with idols, the people deluded and enslaved by the devils using them. Ven. Mary says the Holy Infant Jesus had no sooner entered Egypt when He prayed to His Heavenly Father for the salvation of the people enslaved by the devil. The idols tottered and fell. Bl. Anne Catherine Emmerick also had a vision of the idols falling. One tradition states when the Holy Family came to Heliopolis and the idols toppled, they also fell throughout the rest of Egypt. The Egyptians were struck with wonder at what this could mean, one tradition says

O most watchful Guardian of the Incarnate Son of God, glorious St. Joseph, what toil was your in supporting and waiting upon the Son of the most high God, especially in the flight into Egypt! Yet at the same time, how you did rejoice to have always near you God Himself, and to see the idols of the Egyptians fall prostrate to the ground before Him. By this sorrow and this joy, obtain for us the grace of keeping ourselves in safety from the infernal tyrant, especially by flight from dangerous occasions; may every idol of earthly affection fall from our hearts; may we

----

they still had a vague remembrance of the Prophet Jeremias and his preachings about the true God, and that the false gods would perish from the earth. Tradition also states the High Priest of the Sun at Heliopolis named Aphrodisius went to accost the Holy Family in his wrath, but when he laid eyes on the Holy Infant, the pure Virgin and the humble St. Joseph, he was struck with awe and knew he was in the presence of the One True God, which is why their idols were laid low. He offered the Holy Family hospitality under his roof, but St. Joseph would not accept it and went to a neighbouring village as it was his duty to raise the Holy Infant, however, it is said Aphrodisius remained very kind to them. Tradition states Aphrodisius was eventually taught by St. Paul, became a Christian priest, then Bishop of Béziers in Gaul (France), where he died a martyr at the age of 101. According to the Roman Martyrology, his feast day is celebrated April 28. (Information from the '*Life and Glories of St. Joseph*', Edward Healy Thompson, M.A., Burnes and Oates, London, 1888.)

be wholly employed in serving Jesus and Mary, and for them alone may we live and happily die.

Our Father . . . Hail Mary . . . Glory be . . .

6. Sixth Sorrow: The return from Egypt.

"But hearing that Archelaus was reigning in Judea in place of his father Herod, he was afraid to go there; and being warned in a dream, he withdrew into the region of Galilee." (Matt. 2:22)

Sixth Joy: Life with Jesus and Mary at Nazareth.

"And when they had fulfilled all things prescribed in the Law of the Lord, they returned into Galilee, into their own town of Nazareth." (Luke 2:39)

O glorious St. Joseph, an angel on earth, you did marvel to see the King of Heaven obedient to your commands, but your consolation in bringing Jesus out of the land of Egypt was troubled by your fear of Archelaus; nevertheless, being assured by the Angel, you dwelt in gladness at Nazareth with Jesus and Mary. By this sorrow and this joy, obtain for us that our hearts may be delivered from harmful fears, so that we may rejoice in peace of conscience and may live in safety with Jesus and Mary and may, like you, die in their company.

Our Father . . . Hail Mary . . .Glory be . . .

7. Seventh Sorrow: The loss of the Child Jesus. "And not finding him, they returned to Jerusalem in search of Him" (Luke 2:45)

Seventh Joy: The finding of the Child Jesus in the Temple. "And it came to pass after three days, that they found him in the Temple, sitting in the midst of the teachers, listening to them and asking them questions." (Luke 2:46)

O glorious St. Joseph, pattern of all holiness, when you did lose, through no fault of your own, the Child Jesus, you sought Him sorrowing for the space of three days, until with great joy you did find Him again in the Temple, sitting in the midst of the doctors. By this sorrow and this joy, we supplicate you, with our hearts upon our lips, to keep us from ever having the misfortune to lose Jesus through mortal sin; but if this supreme misfortune should befall us, grant that we may seek Him with unceasing sorrow until we find Him again, ready to show us His great mercy, especially at the hour of death; so that we may pass over to enjoy His presence in Heaven; and there, in company with you, may we sing the praises of His Divine mercy forever.

Our Father . . . Hail Mary . . . Glory be . . .

Antiphon: And Jesus Himself was beginning about the age of thirty years, being (as it was supposed) the Son of Joseph.

V. Pray for us, O holy Joseph.

R. That we may be made worthy of the promises of Christ.

Let Us Pray. O God, Who in Your ineffable Providence did vouchsafe to choose Blessed Joseph to be the spouse of Your most holy Mother, grant, we beseech You, that he whom we venerate as our protector on earth may be our intercessor in Heaven. Who lives and reigns forever and ever. Amen.

❧ ✿ ❧

Traditional Litany to St. Joseph

(Approved by St. Pius X, 1909)

Lord, have mercy on us.
 Christ, have mercy on us.
Lord, have mercy on us.

Christ, hear us.
 Christ, graciously hear us.

God the Father of Heaven, *have mercy on us.*
God the Son, Redeemer of the world,
    have mercy on us.
God the Holy Ghost, *have mercy on us.*
Holy Trinity, One God, *have mercy on us.*
Holy Mary, *pray for us.*
St. Joseph, *pray for us.*
Illustrious son of David, *pray for us.*
Light of patriarchs, *pray for us.*
Spouse of the Mother of God, *pray for us.*
Chaste guardian of the Virgin, *pray for us.*
Foster father of the Son of God, *pray for us.*
Watchful defender of Christ, *pray for us.*
Head of the Holy Family, *pray for us.*

Joseph most just, *pray for us.*
Joseph most chaste, *pray for us.*
Joseph most prudent, *pray for us.*

Joseph most valiant, *pray for us.*
Joseph most obedient, *pray for us.*
Joseph most faithful, *pray for us.*

Mirror of patience, *pray for us.*
Lover of poverty, *pray for us.*
Model of workmen, *pray for us.*
Glory of home life, *pray for us.*
Guardian of virgins, *pray for us.*
Pillar of families, *pray for us.*
Solace of the afflicted, *pray for us.*
Hope of the sick, *pray for us.*
Patron of the dying, *pray for us.*
Terror of demons, *pray for us.*
Protector of Holy Church, *pray for us.*

Lamb of God,
  Who takes away the sins of the world,
      Spare us, O Lord!
Lamb of God,
 Who takes away the sins of the world,
      Graciously hear us, O Lord!
Lamb of God,
 Who takes away the sins of the world,
      Have mercy on us!
   V. He made him the lord of His household,
   R. *And prince over all His possessions.*

Let Us Pray: O God, Who in Thine ineffable Providence didst vouchsafe to choose Blessed Joseph to be the spouse of Thy most holy Mother, grant, we beseech Thee, that he whom we venerate as our protector on earth may be our intercessor in Heaven. Who lives and reigns forever and ever. Amen.

❧ ✽ ❧

Prayer Before Work
to St. Joseph the Worker

(Composed by St. Pius X.)

O Glorious Saint Joseph, model of all those who are devoted to labour, obtain for me the grace to work in a spirit of penance for the expiation of my many sins; to work conscientiously, putting the call of duty above my natural inclinations; to work with thankfulness and joy, considering it an honour to employ and develop by means of labour the gifts received from God; to work with order, peace, moderation, and patience, never shrinking from weariness and trials; to work above all with purity of intention and detachment from self, keeping unceasingly before my eyes death and the account that I must give of time lost, talents unused, good omitted, and vain complacency in success, so fatal to the work of God. All for Jesus, all through Mary, all after thy example, O Patriarch, Saint Joseph. Such shall be my watch-word in life and in death. Amen.

❧ ✽ ❧

The Unfailing or 'Miracle Prayer' to St. Joseph

A Novena Prayer

According to the *Pieta* Prayer book, this prayer dates to the year 50 AD. The book says:

"This prayer was found in the 50th year of our Lord and Saviour Jesus Christ. In 1505, it was sent from the pope to Emperor Charles when he was going into battle. Whoever shall read this prayer or hear it or keep it about themselves, shall never die a sudden death or be drowned, nor shall poison take effect on them; neither shall they fall into the hands of the enemy or be burned in any fire or be overpowered in battle. Say for nine mornings for anything you desire. It has never been known to fail." (This prayer has never been known to fail, as long as it is said in faith and for a particular spiritual benefit for you or for those whom you pray for.)"

(NOTE: The prayer is also prayed as a Novena nine days before the feast of St. Joseph, the novena starting on March 10. This novena was released on September 25, 1950 with the Imprimatur of Hugh C. Boyle, Bishop of Pittsburgh. However, it has been debated that the alleged origins and history of this prayer is spurious - the year 50 AD is a very early date for a published prayer, claimed to have been composed before much of the New Testament that does not contain many mentions about St. Joseph. The claims about the year 50 AD and the Pope and Emperor Charles are not supported, nevertheless it is a beautiful prayer, and since it has been granted an Imprimatur, it has been included in other approved novenas. Heaven always listens to prayers said with love, faith and devotion.)

The Prayer

O St. Joseph, whose protection is so great, so strong, so prompt before the throne of God, I place in you all my interests and desires.

O St. Joseph, do assist me by your powerful intercession, and obtain for me from your Divine Son all spiritual blessings, through Jesus Christ, our Lord. So that, having engaged here below your heavenly power, I may offer my thanksgiving and homage to the most loving of Fathers.

O St. Joseph, I never weary of contemplating you, and Jesus asleep in your arms; I dare not approach while He reposes near your heart. Press Him close in my name and kiss His fine head for me and ask Him to return the kiss when I draw my dying breath.

St. Joseph, patron of departing souls, pray for me. (Mention your intention). Amen.

ॐ❀ॐ

"Ad te beáte Joseph"

Prayer Composed to St. Joseph by Pope Leo XIII

(This prayer to Saint Joseph was composed by Pope Leo XIII in his 1889 encyclical, *Quamquam pluries*. He requested that it be added to the end of the Rosary, especially during the month of October, which is dedicated to the Rosary. The prayer is enriched with a partial indulgence (*Handbook of Indulgences*, conc. 19), and may be said after the *Salve Regina* and concluding prayer. It may also be used to conclude other Marian devotions.)

To thee, O blessed Joseph, do we have recourse in our tribulation, and, having implored the help of thy thrice-holy Spouse, we confidently invoke thy patronage also. By that charity wherewith thou wast united to the immaculate Virgin Mother of God, and by that fatherly affection with which thou didst embrace the Child Jesus, we beseech thee and we humbly pray, that thou wouldst look graciously upon the inheritance which Jesus Christ hath purchased by His Blood, and assist us in our needs by thy power and strength.

Most watchful guardian of the Holy Family, protect the chosen people of Jesus Christ; keep far from us, most loving father, all blight of error and corruption: mercifully assist us from Heaven, most mighty defender, in this our conflict with the powers of darkness; and, even as of old thou didst rescue the Child Jesus from the supreme peril of His life, so now defend God's Holy Church from the snares of the enemy and from all adversity; keep us one and all under thy continual protection, that we may be supported by thine example and thine assistance, may be enabled to lead a holy life, die a happy death and come at last to the possession of everlasting blessedness in Heaven. Amen.

Hail Joseph, Son of David

Hail Joseph Son of David, God is with thee! Blessed art thou amongst men and blessed is Our Lord Jesus Christ!

Holy Joseph, Guardian of the Redeemer, pray for us and be with us, now and as we sigh our last breath.   Amen.

Glorious St. Joseph

Glorious Joseph, kind father and friend,
Humbly to thee myself I commend;
Keep me, watch over me, help and defend.
By virtue's path lead to the heavenly land,
And in my last hour be thou near at hand.
Amen.

Hail Holy Joseph

Hail Holy Joseph! True spouse of Mary, hail!
Chaste as the lily flowing
    in Eden's peaceful vale.

Hail Holy Joseph! Father of Christ esteemed!
Father be thou to those
    thy foster Son redeemed.

Hail Holy Joseph! Prince of the house of God,
may His best graces be
    by thy sweet hands bestowed.

Hail Holy Joseph! Comrade of angels, hail!
Cheer thou the hearts that faint,
    and guide the steps that fail.

Hail Holy Joseph! God's choice wert thou alone,
to thee the Word made flesh
    was subject as a Son.

Hail Holy Joseph! Teach us our flesh to tame,
and Mary, keep the hearts
    that love thy spouse's name.
    Amen.

ȣ❀Ɇ

154

The 'Holy Cloak' of St. Joseph
30 Day Novena

This particular 30 Day Novena also called the 'Holy Cloak of St. Joseph' was composed to honour the thirty years St. Joseph lived with Our Lord and Our Lady. It is obviously an old tradition, as St. Teresa of Avila (1515-1582) attested to to the graces gained from it: "If you really want to believe in it, prove it to yourself by reciting the Novena and you will be finally convinced."

No doubt, the novena was added to and grew over the years, but apparently some sources say the form we have now was popularised by St. Luigi Guanella (1842-1915) who founded the Pious Union of Saint Joseph (1914) with his supporter and first member Pope Pius X. Today, there are numerous people who also give thanks for many graces and petitions granted through the 'Holy Cloak' Novena.

Why is it called the 'Holy Cloak'?

From the petitions in the novena itself, we see that the prayer was offered as a gift of a 'mystic cloak' to St. Joseph, similar to the tradition that as each Hail Mary in the Rosary becomes a rose offered to Our Lady that forms a crown we give in gift to her. Each day of the 'Holy Cloak' novena is said with the intention it is mystically woven into a heavenly cloak as a gift for St. Joseph, and we hope that he is pleased with the gift, will graciously grant our petitions and enclose us in his own holy cloak the same way as Our Lady protects us with her holy mantle.

How to pray the 'Holy Cloak':

* Although the various offerings and prayers are numbered, this appears to be for the sake of simply sectioning them. All the offerings, supplications, prayers, etc. must be said, there is no picking or choosing from the numbers.

* Apparently, it was recommended by St. Teresa and highly efficacious if additional prayers for the Holy Souls in Purgatory are also said with it. It appears these prayers are left to the individual. The 'De Profundis' has been suggested, also other prayers to help the Holy Souls, etc.

*If you miss a day of the Novena, you may make up the missing day by reciting it on the last day, i.e. the 30th Day, of the Novena. For example if you missed two days, you can say those two on the last day, as well as the prayers for that day. (However it is not recommended you miss many days as the Novena itself is long, we are attempting to 'weave' a cloak after all!)

THE PRAYERS

In the name of the Father, and of the Son, and of the Holy Spirit. Amen.

Jesus, Mary and Joseph, I give Thee my heart and my soul.

(Recite the Glory Be 3 times to our Heavenly Father in thanksgiving for having exalted St. Joseph to a position of such exceptional dignity.)

OFFERING

(1) O Glorious Patriarch St. Joseph, I

humbly prostrate myself before Thee. I beg the Lord Jesus, thine Immaculate Spouse, the Blessed Virgin Mary, and all the Angels and Saints in the Heavenly Court, to join me in this devotion. I offer thee this precious cloak, while pledging my sincerest faith and devotion. I promise to do all in my power to honour thee throughout my lifetime to prove my love for thee.

Help me, St. Joseph. Assist me now and throughout my lifetime, but especially at the moment of my death, as thou wert assisted by Jesus and Mary, that I may join thee one day in Heaven and there honour thee for all eternity. Amen.

(2) O Glorious Patriarch St. Joseph, prostrate, before thee and thy Divine Son, Jesus, I offer thee, with heartfelt devotion, this precious treasury of prayers, being ever mindful of the numerous virtues which adorned thy sacred person. In thee, O Glorious Patriarch, was fulfilled the dream of thy precursor the first Joseph, who indeed seemed to have been sent by God to prepare the way for thy presence on this Earth. In fact, not only wert thou surrounded by the shining splendour of the rays of the Divine Sun, Jesus,

but thou wert splendidly reflected in the brilliant light of the mystic moon, the Blessed Virgin Mary. O Glorious Patriarch, if the example of the ancient Jacob, who personally went to congratulate his favourite son, who was exalted on the throne of Egypt, served to bring all his progeny there, should not the example of Jesus and Mary, who honoured thee with their greatest respect and trust, serve to bring me, thy devoted servant, to present thee with this precious cloak in thy honour.

Grant, O Great St. Joseph, that the Almighty God may turn a benevolent glance toward me. As the ancient Joseph did not reject his guilty and cruel brothers, but rather accepted them with love and protected and saved them from hunger and death, I beseech thee, O Glorious Patriarch, through thine intercession, grant that the Lord may never abandon me in this exiled valley of sorrows. Grant that He may always number me as one of thy devoted servants who dost live serenely under the patronage of thy Holy Cloak. Grant that I may live always within the protection of this patronage, every day of my life and particularly at that moment when I draw my dying breath.

PRAYERS

(1): Hail O Glorious St. Joseph, thou who art entrusted with the priceless treasures of Heaven and Earth and foster-father of Him Who doth nourish all the creatures of the universe. Thou art, after Mary, the Saint most worthy of our love and devotion. Thou alone, above all the Saints, wert chosen for that supreme honour of rearing, guiding, nourishing and even embracing the Messiah, Whom so many kings and prophets would have so desired to behold.

St. Joseph, save my soul and obtain for me from the Divine Mercy of God that petition for which I humbly pray. And for the Holy Souls in Purgatory, grant a great comfort from their pain.

(Recite the Glory Be 3 times to our Heavenly Father in thanksgiving for having exalted St. Joseph to a position of such exceptional dignity.)

(2) O powerful St. Joseph, thou wert proclaimed the Patron of the Universal Church, therefore, I invoke thee, above all the other Saints, as the greatest protector of the

afflicted, and I offer countless blessings to thy most generous heart, always ready to help in any need.

To thee, O Glorious St. Joseph, come the widows, the orphans, the abandoned, the afflicted, the oppressed. There is no sorrow, heartache or anguish which thou hast not consoled. Deign, I beseech thee, to use on my behalf those gifts which God hast given thee, until I too shall be granted the answer to my petition. And thou, Holy Souls in Purgatory, pray to St. Joseph for me.

(Recite the Glory Be 3 times to our Heavenly Father in thanksgiving for having exalted St. Joseph to a position of such exceptional dignity.)

(3). Countless are those who have prayed to thee before me and have received comfort and peace, graces and favours. My heart, so sad and sorrowful, cannot find rest in the midst of this trial which besets me. O Glorious St. Joseph, thou knowest all my needs even before I set them forth in prayer. Thou knowest how important this petition is for me. I prostrate myself before thee as I sigh under the heavy weight of the problem which confronts me.

There is no human heart in which I can confide my sorrow; and even if I should find a compassionate creature who would be willing to assist me, still he would be unable to help me. Only thou can help me in my sorrow, St. Joseph, and I beg thee to hear my plea.

Has not St. Teresa left it written in her dialogues that the world may always know "Whatever you ask of St. Joseph, you shall receive."

O St. Joseph, comforter of the afflicted, have pity on my sorrow and pity on those Poor Souls who place so much hope in their prayers to thee.

(Recite the Glory Be 3 times to our Heavenly Father in thanksgiving for having exalted St. Joseph to a position of such exceptional dignity.)

(4). O Sublime Patriarch St. Joseph, because of thy perfect obedience to God, thou mayest intercede for me.
For thy holy life full of grace and merit, hear my prayer.
For thy most sweet name, help me. For your most holy tears, comfort me.
For thy seven sorrows, intercede for me.

For your seven joys, console me.

From all harm of body and soul, deliver me. From all danger and disaster, save me. Assist me with thy powerful intercession and seek for me, through thy power and mercy, all that is necessary for my salvation and particularly the favour of which I now stand in such great need.

(Recite the Glory Be 3 times to our Heavenly Father in thanksgiving for having exalted St. Joseph to a position of such exceptional dignity.)

(5) O Glorious St. Joseph, countless are the graces and favours which thou hast obtained for afflicted souls. Illness of every nature, those who are oppressed, persecuted, betrayed, bereft of all human comfort, even those in need of their life bread- all who imploreth thy powerful intercession are comforted in their affliction.

Do not permit, O dearest St. Joseph, that I alone be the only one of all who hast appealed to thee, to be denied this petition which I so earnestly beg of thee. Show thy kindness and generosity even to me, that I may cry out in thanksgiving, "Eternal glory to our Holy Patriarch St. Joseph, my great protector on Earth and the defender of the Holy Souls in Purgatory."

(Recite the Glory Be 3 times to our Heavenly Father in thanksgiving for having exalted St. Joseph to a position of such exceptional dignity.)

(6) Eternal Father, Who art in Heaven, through the merits of Jesus and Mary, I beg Thee to grant my petition. In the name of Jesus and Mary I prostrate myself before Thy Divine presence and I beseech Thee to accept my hopeful plea to persevere in my prayers that I may be numbered among the throngs of those who live under the patronage of St. Joseph.

Extend Thy blessing on this precious treasury of prayers which I today offer to him as a pledge of my devotion.

(Recite the Glory Be 3 times to our Heavenly Father in thanksgiving for having exalted St. Joseph to a position of such exceptional dignity.)

SUPPLICATIONS in honour of St. Joseph's hidden life with JESUS and MARY

St. Joseph, pray that Jesus may come into my
soul and sanctify me.
St. Joseph, pray that Jesus may come into my
heart and inspire it with charity.
St. Joseph, pray that Jesus may come into my
mind and enlighten it.
St. Joseph, pray that Jesus may guide my will
and strengthen it.
St. Joseph, pray that Jesus may direct my
thoughts and purify them.
St. Joseph, pray that Jesus may guide my
desires and direct them.
St. Joseph, pray that Jesus may look upon my
deeds and extend His blessings.
St. Joseph, pray that Jesus may inflame me
with love for Him.
St. Joseph, request for me from Jesus
the imitation of thy virtues.
St. Joseph, request for me from Jesus
true humility of spirit.
St. Joseph, request for me from Jesus
meekness of heart.
St. Joseph, request for me from Jesus
peace of soul.
St. Joseph, request for me from Jesus
a holy fear of the Lord.

St. Joseph, request for me from Jesus
a desire for perfection.
St. Joseph, request for me from Jesus
a gentleness of heart.
St. Joseph, request for me from Jesus
a pure and charitable heart.
St. Joseph, request for me from Jesus
the wisdom of faith.
St. Joseph, request for me from Jesus
His blessing of perseverance
in my good deeds.
St. Joseph, request for me from Jesus
the strength to carry my crosses.
St. Joseph, request for me from Jesus
a disdain for the material goods of this world.
St. Joseph, request for me from Jesus
the grace to always walk on the narrow path
toward Heaven.
St. Joseph, request for me from Jesus
the grace to avoid all occasion of sin.
St. Joseph, request for me from Jesus
a holy desire for eternal bliss.
St. Joseph, request for me from Jesus
the grace of final perseverance.

St. Joseph, do not abandon me.
St. Joseph, pray that my heart
may never cease to love thee
and that my lips may ever praise thee.

St. Joseph, for the love
thou didst bear for Jesus,
grant that I may learn to love Him.
St. Joseph, graciously accept me
as thy devoted servant.
St. Joseph, I give myself to thee;
accept my pleas and hear my prayers.
St. Joseph, do not abandon me
at the hour of my death.
Jesus, Mary and Joseph,
I give Thee my heart and my soul.

(Recite the Glory Be 3 times, etc.)

INVOCATIONS TO SAINT JOSEPH

(1) Remember O most chaste spouse of the
Blessed Virgin Mary, my good protector St.
Joseph, that never was it known that anyone
who didst come to thy protection, and sought
thine intercession was left unaided.
Confidently I prostrate myself before thee and
fervently beg for thy powerful intervention. O
foster-Father of our dear Redeemer, despise
not my petition, but in thy mercy, hear and
answer me. Amen.

(2) Glorious St. Joseph, spouse of the Blessed Virgin Mary and virginal father of Jesus, look upon me and watch over me; lead me on the path of sanctifying grace; take heed of the urgent needs which I now beg thee to envelop within the folds of thy fatherly cloak. Dismiss those obstacles and difficulties standing in the way of my prayer and grant that the happy answer to my petition may serve for the greater glory of God and my eternal salvation.

As a pledge of my undying gratitude, I promise to spread the word of thy glory whilst offering thanks to the Lord for having so blest thy power and might in Heaven and on earth.

(* NOW RECITE THE LITANY of ST. JOSEPH – turn to page 144, then say the closing prayers below.)

CLOSING PRAYER OF THE HOLY CLOAK

O Glorious Patriarch St. Joseph, thou who wert chosen by God above all men to be the earthly head of the most holy of families, I beseech thee to accept me within the folds of thy holy cloak, that thou mayest become the guardian and custodian of my soul.

From this moment on, I choose thee as my father, my protector, my counsellor, my patron and I beseech thee to place in thy custody my body, my soul, all that I am, all that I possess, my life and my death.

Look upon me as one of thy children; defend me from the treachery of my enemies, invisible or otherwise, assist me at all times in all my necessities; console me in the bitterness of my life, and especially at the hour of my death. Say but one word for me to the Divine Redeemer Whom thou wert deemed worthy to hold in thine arms, and to the Blessed Virgin Mary, thy most chaste spouse. Request for me those blessings which will lead me to salvation. Include me amongst those who art most dear to thee and I shall set forth to prove myself worthy of thy special patronage. Amen.

CLOSING PRAYER TO SAINT JOSEPH

To thee do we cry in our tribulations, O Blessed Saint Joseph, as we confidently invoke thy patronage, after that of thy most holy spouse, the Blessed Virgin Mary.

By that sacred bond of devotion which linked thee to the Immaculate Virgin, Mother of God, and for the fatherly love thou didst lavish on the child Jesus, we beg thee to cast a glance on those heavenly gifts which the Divine Redeemer hast obtained for all mankind through His Precious Blood and through thy power and mercy, help us in our needs.

O holy protector of the holy family, protect us children of the Lord Jesus Christ; keep far from us the errors and evils which corrupt the world; assist us from Heaven in our struggles against the powers of darkness. And as thou once didst protect the Divine Child from the cruel edict of Herod, now defend the Church and keep it safe from all dangers and threats; spread over all of us thy holy patronage so that by following thine example and aided by thy spiritual guidance, we may all aspire to a virtuous life, look to a holy death and secure for ourselves the blessing of eternal happiness in Heaven. Amen.

End of the Holy Cloak Novena

⊰❀⊱

Prayer to Obtain a Conversion

O glorious Patriarch St. Joseph, thou who merited to be called 'just' by the Holy Ghost, I urgently recommend to the soul of (Name), which Jesus redeemed at the price of His Precious Blood. Thou knowest how deplorable is the state and how unhappy the life of those who have banished this loving Saviour from their hearts, and how greatly they are exposed to the danger of losing Him eternally. Permit not, I beseech thee, that a soul so dear to me should continue any longer in its evil ways; preserve it from the danger that threatens it; touch the heart of the prodigal child and conduct (him/her) back to the bosom of the fondest of fathers. Do not abandon (him/her), I implore thee, till thou hast opened to (him/her) the gates of the Heavenly city, where (he/she) will praise and bless thee throughout eternity for the happiness which (he/she) will owe to thy powerful intercession. Amen.

ൟ ❀ ൟ

Prayer to St. Joseph to Obtain Light upon Choosing a State of Life

Great Saint, who wast so docile to the leading of the Holy Ghost, obtain for me grace to know to what state Providence has destined me. Do not permit me to err in this important choice upon which depends my happiness in this world, and perhaps my eternal salvation, but obtain for me the grace, that enlightened concerning the Divine Will and being faithful in following it, I may walk in the way that the Lord has determined for me, which will conduct me to a blessed eternity. Amen.

಄ ❀ ಄

Prayer for Purity

Saint Joseph, father and guardian of virgins, to whose faithful keeping Christ Jesus, innocence itself, and Mary, the Virgin of virgins was entrusted, I pray and beseech you by that twofold and most precious charge, by Jesus and Mary, to save me from all uncleanness, to keep my mind untainted, my heart pure, and my body chaste; and to help me always to serve Jesus and Mary in perfect chastity. Amen.

Prayer to Obtain a Special Request

O Blessed Saint Joseph, tender-hearted father, faithful guardian of Jesus, chaste spouse of the Mother of God, we pray and beseech thee to offer to God the Father His Divine Son, bathed in blood on the cross for sinners, and through the thrice-holy Name of Jesus, obtain for us from the Eternal Father, the favour we implore. (*Mention your request.*) Appease the Divine anger so justly inflamed by our crimes; beg of Jesus mercy for thy children. Amid the splendours of eternity, forget not the sorrows of those who suffer, those who pray, those who weep. Stay the Almighty arm which smites us, that by thy prayers and those of thy most holy spouse, the Heart of Jesus may be moved to pity and to pardon. Joseph, pray for us. Amen.

The Nine First Wednesdays Devotion

Promoted by the Pious Union of St. Joseph

Wednesday has traditionally been the day devoted to St. Joseph. What better way to honour the foster father of Our Lord and his chaste heart that loved Jesus and Mary than by following the example of the Nine First Fridays Devotion to the Sacred Heart?

Make Nine First Wednesdays in honour of St. Joseph for the grace of a happy death for yourself and the ones dear to you. As charity is the best way to be worthy of the grace of a happy death, offer the First Wednesday Mass and Communion and devotions in honour of St. Joseph for nine consecutive months, and in a special way for the salvation of the dying, especially for an undying sinner who is in danger of losing their soul for all Eternity without the grace of final repentance. The Lord rewards those who honour His foster Father who took care of Him on earth, and, whatever St. Joseph asks, it is not refused.

Help a soul achieve a happy death and the same grace will most certainly not be refused you.

A Short Prayer for the Dying

O St. Joseph, foster father of the Child Jesus and true spouse of the Blessed Virgin Mary, pray for us and for the dying of this day (or this night). Amen.

QUOTES from the SAINTS:

St. Teresa of Avila on St. Joseph

"I only beg, for the love of God, that anyone who does not believe me will put what I say to the test, and he will see by experience what great advantages come from his commending himself to this glorious patriarch and having devotion to him. Those who practice prayer should have a special affection for him always. I do not know how anyone can think of the Queen of the Angels, during the time that she suffered so much with the Child Jesus, without giving thanks to Saint Joseph for the way he helped them. If anyone cannot find a master to teach him how to pray, let him take this glorious saint as his master and he will not go astray."

❧✿☙

Our Lord to St. Margaret Mary

"I wish that every day you offer special prayers to Our mother and St. Joseph, Our most sweet guardian."

Our Lady to Ven. Mary de Agreda

"You must see to it that you continually increase your love and devotion to this great Saint. In all your necessities, you must avail yourself of his protection, under all circumstances you must encourage as many people as possible toward this devotion . . . for indeed, whatever our devoted spouse requests in Heaven, the Almighty God will grant on Earth."

❧ ✾ ❧

St. Thomas Aquinas

"Some Saints are privileged to extend to us their patronage with particular efficacy in certain needs but not in others, but our holy patron St Joseph has the power to assist us in all cases, in every necessity, in every undertaking."

St. Alphonsus de Ligouri

"Go then to Joseph and do
all that he shall say to you.
Go to Joseph and obey him,
as Jesus and Mary obeyed him.
Go to Joseph and speak to him,
as they spoke to him.
Go to Joseph and consult him,
as they consulted him.
Go to Joseph and honour him,
as they honoured him.
Go to Joseph and be grateful to him,
as they were grateful to him.
Go to Joseph and love him,
as they love him still."

❧❀❧

"Can we find such another man,
that is full of the spirit of God? …
Go to Joseph, and do all that he shall say to you."

(Genesis 41: 38, 55)

Illustration Credits

Cover and Page 28 - 'St. Joseph and the Christ Child', Leopold Kupelwieser (1796-1862). Art Institute of Chicago.

Page 41 - 'The Dream of St. Joseph', Anonymous, (early 18th century). Metropolitan Museum of Art.

Page 56 - 'Holy Family', after Reni by Anonymous, (c. 1680-1738). Metropolitan Museum of Art.

Page 64 - 'The Presentation of Christ in the Temple' from 'The Life of the Virgin', (c. 1504-1505) by Albrecht Dürer (1471-1528). Cleveland Museum of Art.

Page 71 – 'Holy Family' by Giorgione (c. 1500). Samuel H. Kress Collection courtesy of the National Gallery of Art / NGA Images.

Page 76 - 'St. Joseph Carrying the Christ Child on the Flight into Egypt', Giulian Tranallesi (1760-1800). Metropolitan Museum of Art.

Page 87 -'The Return to Nazareth', Francesco Conti (1735). Cleveland Museum of Art.

Page 92 – 'Holy Family with a Bird', Simon Vouet (1590-1649). Art Institute of Chicago.

Page 113 – 'Holy Family', painting after a traditional picture, Anonymous (c. 2000).

Page 128 – 'Flight into Egypt', after a painting by Reni by Anonymous (1640-1678). Metropolitan Museum of Art.

Page 145 – 'St. Joseph and the Christ Child', Anonymous (17th Century). Metropolitan Museum of Art.

Page 154 – 'St. Joseph', Anonymous, (date?). Metropolitan Museum of Art.

Page 172 – 'Adoration of the Shepherds', Simão Rodrigues (1605).

Page 180 – 'Saint Joseph portant l'Enfant Jésus', (19th century), Octave Nicolas François Tassaert (1800-1874). Paris Musées – Petit Palais, Musée dea Beaux-arts de la Ville de Paris (DUTI762)